" live to learn, le[...]
  you'll love to [...]

" The successful people make it a habit
  of doing things failures don't like
  to do —

High Fives
and High Hopes

EFy 90'

High Fives
and High Hopes

*Favorite Talks
Especially
for Youth*

Deseret Book Company
Salt Lake City, Utah

Special appreciation is expressed to the contributors to this work for their willingness to share their thoughts and testimonies with youth. Each author accepts complete personal responsibility for the material contained within his or her chapter. There is no endorsement for this work (real or implied) by The Church of Jesus Christ of Latter-day Saints, the Church Educational System, or Brigham Young University.

Library of Congress Catalog Card Number 90-81267

ISBN 0-87579-356-8

Printed in the United States of America

10 9 8 7 6 5 4 3 2 1

Contents

v

CONTENTS

Chapter 1

Follow, Follow Me— Prophets, Patriarchs, and Heroes

Scott Anderson

Have you ever driven in the fog? Isn't that an interesting challenge? How do you stay on the road in the fog? In some states you have help—you have some bumps on the side of the road. When you hit those bumps, you know it's time to go the other direction. Some other states don't have any bumps. Oh, they do, but not in the right places—they're all in the middle of the road and everywhere else.

When driving through snow and fog, what can keep us on the road? The wonderful little white lines. Our lives are a little like driving in the fog. Lehi, sharing a representation of life, said that a mist of darkness comes over us and we need to get through it somehow. Driving along through the fog of life, we learn line upon line. Scriptures, commandments, parents, bishops, and the living prophets all help us learn line upon line.

What about those times when the fog gets really dense and we can see only a few lines ahead? Have you ever been in that much fog? Once I learned a lesson about that while driving to the airport. I was in a hurry. The fog was so dense that the fastest I could go was twenty miles an hour. All of a sudden a huge semi truck went by with its fog lights on. I quickly found that I could go a lot faster following him than I could just traveling on my own. So, I pulled in behind the truck and was able to go forty-five and fifty—just roaring

1

along. My only problem was that I was going to end up wherever he was going.

My mom was driving through the fog one night, going to a study group. She and her friends decided they would follow someone who knew the way because they couldn't find their way through the fog. Twelve cars were following the lead car. The leader pulled up to a stop sign and turned right. There was another car just like his that was stopped, and it went straight. All twelve cars ended up following the wrong car. As they pulled through the intersection, the driver of the lead car looked in his rear-view mirror and saw twelve cars following him. He pulled into his subdivision, and all the cars turned and followed him. He must have watched too much television, because he decided that the Mafia was after him! He drove around just as fast as he could trying to lose those cars. He sped up, and the twelve cars behind him sped up. They went all around the subdivision until finally the lead driver saw a house with its lights on. Gambling that the people might be home, he decided to run in and call the police. He pulled up next to the house, ran up to the porch, and started to beat on the door. Nobody was home—that's why they had all the lights on. He was standing there, pounding on the door, and all he could hear was all the cars stopping and footsteps coming through the fog. My mom was one of the first ones through the fog, and she heard him say, "No, no, please don't kill me." She came home laughing. They never did make it to the study group.

In our lives, there is someone with spiritual fog lights on. He can see clearly enough to give us exact, careful direction, and we can then understand things we wouldn't know on our own. He is the living Prophet.

Our prophets see far enough ahead that they remind us to lengthen our stride and quicken our pace. We have so many things to do. I picture the Prophet driving a spiritual Porsche. He travels at about two hundred miles an hour down the freeway of life. He then turns to us and says, "Lengthen your stride! Quicken your pace!" And we're standing on our skateboards or tricycles saying, "Well, I'm trying. I'm trying." We need to follow his tail lights, if you will, and, seeing his example, give everything we have to try to stay up with him. If we do this, we are going to be ready for the challenges of life. If we don't, we're not. I have strong feelings about the importance of active obedience.

Is it easy to follow a prophet? Has it *ever* been easy to follow a prophet? I think we need to consider this, because many times in history following a prophet has been a challenge.

Let's look at an example out of those beautiful books, the scriptures. Once there was a great young man named Gideon. He was probably about your age. The Lord called him to be the Prophet of Israel. He said, "Me? The Prophet?" The Lord assured him that he had great potential. So Gideon worked to strengthen his testimony. He worked to get his own confirmation. Then he received his first assignment. The Lord asked him to go out to a grove, chop down all the trees, and burn down all the idols there. Any of you who have read the Old Testament know that people used to do awful things with these idols in the groves. They had an idol called Moloch and one called Baal. Baal worship included torture and immorality. Moloch was a metal image that would be stoked up until it was red hot like a furnace. The people would sacrifice their little children to Moloch. So, the Lord sent this young man to cleanse the groves. The scriptures say that he took ten of his friends and did as the Lord had commanded. I think that was probably one of the best young adult parties they ever had. They had a big fire and maybe even a cook-out.

The next day, the people from the city went out to worship the idols, but they couldn't do it any more—which I am so thankful for. A knock came on Gideon's door, and Gideon's dad answered it. There stood the people from town, saying, "Bring Gideon out here." Gideon's dad said, "Why do you want Gideon?"

"He destroyed our god last night."

Gideon's father just looked at them and said, "He did *what*? My boy? I didn't know he had that kind of power. You have always told me your god was all powerful. Isn't that right?"

"Yes. That's right. Baal *is* all powerful."

The father said, "You don't have to punish Gideon. If he destroyed Baal, certainly Baal will come and get my son."

They said, "Okay. Baal on your son," and away they went.

Gideon's father walked back into the house and said something like, "Put her there, Gideon. Give me five. All right!" Things seemed okay. Baal didn't seem to be doing anything, and Gideon was fine.

Soon, however, the massive army of the Midianites would come over the mountains to destroy Israel. But the Israelites had a prophet they could follow. Gideon was called to lead them, and this was going to be a big challenge for them. This was really the first time they had ever followed Gideon.

Gideon gathered the biggest army he could—32,000 soldiers to fight an army of 135,000. That is a big army! Imagine that we are Gideon's army and that tomorrow we're going over the mountains to fight. There are 135,000 of the Midianites, and there are only 32,000 of us—are you ready? The odds are just four to one—can you handle that?

Gideon said to the Israelites, "We need to go defend our families." Then Gideon received a message from the Lord: "Gideon, you have too many soldiers." It's a good thing the Lord didn't tell *me* that. I would have said, "Have you counted the Midianite soldiers? Maybe they're the ones who have too many." But not Gideon; he just said, "All right. What do you want me to do?"

The Lord said, "Tell your soldiers that if any of them are afraid to die, they are to go home." So Gideon said to the 32,000 Israelites, "If any of you are afraid to die and want to live past tomorrow, I want you to go home right now. If you want to see your families again and aren't ready to give your life, leave." Twenty-two thousand went home. He now had 10,000. Can you picture Gideon gathering the 10,000 together and saying, "Everything is all right. Yes, I know that two-thirds of our army just went home, but you're the strong ones; you're the stalwart. There are 135,000 of the enemy, but the 10,000 of us with the Lord's help can handle them. Everything will be fine." Now what are the odds? They're getting worse! "That's okay, you take your fourteen, you take fourteen, and everything will be fine." Would it be easy to follow the Prophet then? Would you wonder about him? Would it be hard when you'd never followed him before?

As if that wasn't challenging enough, Gideon received another message from the Lord: "There are still too many. Send some more home." Gideon took his troops to the brook for a drink. Some of them dropped their weapons to drink, while others held their weapons and drank carefully. All those who dropped their weapons, Gideon sent home. The ones that held their weapons and drank carefully, he kept. Nine thousand seven hundred went home. Gideon now had 300 soldiers. He announced: "Okay, tonight we're going to march over the mountain to fight 135,000 Midianites." How would you feel?

Gideon then proclaimed. "The Lord's going to be with us. I have received instructions from him about how we're going to fight: Bring your lanterns tonight and cover them with water pitchers so nobody can see the light. Also, bring your trumpets. Meet here." A soldier raised his hand and said, "I know my music's bad, but it's not going to kill them, Gideon." Would that take a little faith?

Picture yourself with a lantern in one hand and a trumpet in the other. Gideon marches you over the mountain, and there are 135,000 trained warriors sleeping. You and your 300 friends are positioned around the camp, just twenty feet from the tents. In one hand, you have a lantern with a pitcher over it; in the other, you have a trumpet. Gideon runs by and says,

5

"When I give you the high sign, uncover your lantern so everybody can see you. Then blow your trumpet for all you're worth." Then he starts walking away. That's his last instruction.

I have mentally put myself twenty feet from that tent so many times, and I have thought, "Could I ever do it?" Imagine yourself blowing your trumpet—then all of a sudden 135,000 soldiers jump out of their tents with their swords. What do you *say?* "Hi! Just wanted to give you a little entertainment. Want an encore? I know another number. You don't like to dance?" What would *you* do? Can you imagine? Would it take some faith? Has it *ever* been easy to follow a prophet? It's *never* been easy, and it wasn't easy for them.

There they stood with their lanterns, and Gideon, the great leader that he was, held up his lantern. He didn't just take off the pitcher, he smashed it! He grabbed his trumpet and blew, and then (I love this part) the three hundred trumpets blared all at once. If the soldiers hadn't blown the trumpets, they would have died. But they followed the Prophet, as hard as it was. Three hundred soldiers uncovered their lanterns and blew their trumpets for all they were worth.

A single trumpeter used to go in front of a battalion of soldiers. Suddenly, the Midianites heard *three hundred* trumpets, and they must have thought three hundred battalions were descending on them. They jumped up, grabbed their swords (no time to put on their armor), and started to fight. Who were they fighting? Each other. Imagine them looking at each other and saying, "Boy, you look familiar." While they were having this battle, the greatest pep band in history was out there playing away on their trumpets. After fighting against themselves, the Midianites began to run away from themselves, and that's a long way to run! As they ran away, the three hundred Israelites could now sing with real meaning, "We Thank Thee, O God, for a Prophet." They had protected their families by following a prophet. It wasn't easy for them, and it won't be easy for you. At times it will be a real struggle.

Now a modern-day example. Once my friends and I went to a fireside. Spencer W. Kimball was coming to talk to us. He wasn't the president of the Church then, but he was a member of the Quorum of the Twelve, so we sustained him as a prophet, seer, and revelator. He was going to talk about dating, courtship, and marriage. We loved to talk about that subject!

Elder Kimball said, "Those of you who are so young should not be dating *at all*." Suddenly all the Beehives were weeping, wailing, and gnashing their teeth. The Scouts were cheering and saying, "Who would want to date? Those girls crawled out of the swamp!" Next, Elder Kimball proclaimed, "Those of you who are older should not be going steady so young." Now the Laurels and priests were getting a little bit on edge. They murmured, "Oh, don't talk about this. My parents are here! Talk about something else." Elder Kimball continued with words something like these: "It is not wise to stay out alone late with nothing else to do but 'huggy bear, kissy-face.' "

At this point, I would like to suggest how to follow this part of the Prophet's counsel. Just carry your scriptures with you at all times. That might be why those pocket-sized editions were printed. If your date stops the car and starts to slide across the seat toward you, just pull out your scriptures and ask, "Oh, did you want to read?" If you need a specific reference, quickly look up Mosiah 13:3 and read aloud, "Touch me not, for God shall smite you if ye lay your hands upon me." If this doesn't work, you could quickly yawn and state, "Oh, I'm sorry, but this mononucleosis is really getting me down!" If this doesn't get the message across, just get out of the car, run around to the driver's side, and say, "Oh, did you want me to drive?"

Now, Elder Kimball didn't just give us a list of no-no's. He also had some positive suggestions. His next statement was, "I have some counsel for you. I think you ought to try group dating." We looked at each other and thought, "Group dating? *Group dating*? Ah, two girls and me. Group dating! Okay, this is going to be great!" I was all for it. Then suddenly I figured out that wasn't what he meant.

He was talking to us about going out in a group and having the strength of numbers to encourage each other to be good. Why be alone and put yourself on the devil's ground? Why stay out so late? Instead, get together in big groups, build positive memories, and have a great time. It sounded good, but my friends were saying, "That might have worked for Brother Kimball in Arizona at the turn of the century, but it won't work today." I think they pictured the kids at school going to the next dance in the farm truck, all grouped together.

We enjoyed Elder Kimball's talk, but we were having some trouble translating it into our actual activities. The next week, however, our bishop walked into our priests quorum meeting and asked how many of us had heard Elder Kimball at the fireside. Then he reminded us that a stake dance was scheduled for that weekend. He expressed his feeling that our stake dances had not been very good, and then he asked, "Do you know why?" We said, "Yes, we do. We have ugly girls in our stake!" The bishop didn't like that answer because his daughter, of course, was in our stake. He announced, "That's not it, brethren. It is because you are not group dating at the stake dances. So, I would like to challenge each of you to dance with at least ten different girls during the next stake dance." One priest replied, "I can't. I don't know how to dance." Having watched this priest at the last dance, the bishop agreed. But then he gave us the tools we needed to follow his counsel—he taught us how to dance. He said, "I have been watching *American Bandstand* this week, and I think the kids on that show pretend they just jumped out of the shower and are drying off. To dance, just pretend you have a towel. Flip it over your back, like this. (To our dismay, he demonstrated as he talked.) Then you grab it behind your

8

back with your other hand and just use it to dry off." We would have agreed to do anything just to get him to stop his demonstration, so we committed to dance with at least ten different girls at the next dance.

Then came the night when we would try to follow a prophet's counsel and apply our bishop's advice. However, there were some challenges at our stake dances. All the girls would stand against one wall in a huge mob and just talk to each other. All the guys would stand next to the refreshments in a big mob and eat all night long. Then a few of the kids who were going steady would walk out to the middle of the floor and go into "the clutch." And they'd say, "Turn down the lights, turn down the lights." All the leaders would walk around with six-inch rulers, saying, "You're dancing too close, you're dancing too close." This dance was about the same. I felt bad, because I had had fifteen showers that week practicing my dance technique. But the mob of girls was over there, and we were over here. It was kind of hard to walk across the floor and ask one of the mob to dance. We would have to walk across the room all alone and say, "Hey, you. No, not you, you! Yeah, you back there. Do you want to dance?" Just scary!

So we were standing around, nobody was dancing much, and finally Jim walked in. He was in our priests quorum, and he said, "Hey, you guys, come on, let's dance." One of the guys said, "No thanks, Jim, I'd rather dance with a girl." He said, "That's not what I meant. Let's all go ask them to dance at the same time. Let's all walk over together, and then it won't be so scary." So twenty of us left the wall and walked over together. Every chaperone in the place sat up, wondering what was going on. As we arrived in front of the mob, Jim said, "Hey, all you girls, come out here and dance." A bunch of them came right out and thought that was a neat idea. Some of the others stood back and said, "No. I want a personal invitation." So a couple of the football players went back and picked up one of the girls by the hands and the feet and said,

"Okay, one, two . . . " and then all the girls came right out. They thought that was personal enough.

Fifty girls came out to dance, and there were twenty of us. But that was okay. We just stood in a big circle together, and if any of the kids stopped dancing, someone would grab them and throw them in the middle of the circle. Everybody would lock shoulders, and the kids in the middle couldn't get out. Then they would have to do some crazy thing. So nobody stopped dancing all night. We had more participation than ever before. Everyone had a great time! I'd had my first group date. I thought, "This is marvelous!"

Two weeks later, school ended, and it seemed like everything else ended too. If you weren't going steady, you just had a boring summer and tried again next year. But not this summer. Because of a prophet's counsel and some wonderful Laurels who decided to follow it, we got an invitation in the mail. The girls said, "We're planning a group date. Would you come over, please?" My buddies were asked to the group date too, and we were pretty excited about going to find out what it was going to be. As we arrived at the party, there were forty or fifty of us in the backyard. There was plenty of good food, so we knew it was going to be a great party. As the guys stood around the refreshments, a few of the girls came around drawing numbers out of a hat and handing them out. When everybody had a number, they announced, "We have our cars parked out in front. They have numbers on the windows. Go jump in the car that has the number you have in your hand." We stuffed food in our pockets, and out we went. Seven of us were packed into the little compact car in which I was jammed. The girls handed us two bags through the window. One was full of numbered balloons, and one was full of all kinds of equipment. Then they proclaimed, "Just pop the numbered balloons in order, one at a time; they have instructions inside. Use the equipment and have a great time. Don't exceed the speed limit—somebody's watching your speedometer. Good-bye!" We found the first balloon

10

and popped it. We found out right then that a girl sitting in the front seat could not stand to have balloons popped. When we popped it, she just shrieked. She jumped too high and made a sun roof where there wasn't one. We finally found the clue; it said, "Go to JB's restaurant and eat a piece of strawberry pie." I volunteered. I said, "I'll sacrifice my body and do this thing." Then the others said "You've got to wear this old, ugly nightshirt and a big blindfold and go into JB's and eat the piece of strawberry pie." It was 9:30 on Saturday night, and the place was packed with people. I said, "I'm sure that Shelly would love to do this!" She volunteered.

We roared down to JB's. The nightshirt went on. Shelly put on the blindfold and stumbled into the restaurant. Everybody was staring at her. She sat down at the counter, and the waitress brought her a piece of strawberry pie — delicious pie with a huge strawberry in front and lots of whipped cream on top. Without being able to see, she picked up half of the pie with her fork and propelled it toward her face. It was obvious to everybody that she would never get it all in. The whole restaurant went quiet, and the people just stared with their mouths open. The pie went "splat," all over her face. We all started to laugh, and then she started to laugh, and then she inhaled. Guess where the whipped cream went. Right up her nose! She was just dying on the spot, and we were dying laughing. All of a sudden another nightshirted victim came wandering in with another group. We grabbed the pie and gobbled it down and grabbed her and threw her in the car and popped the next balloon. "Eek!" the girl in front screamed.

We grabbed the second clue, which said to go over to the movie theater and get a pizza box. We roared over to the drive-in and realized that with seven of us in the car it was going to cost us eighteen dollars to get in. We didn't have that kind of money, so my friends elected me to walk into the drive-in. Have you ever walked into a drive-in movie theater? It's really interesting. I said, "One ticket please." The

11

teller said, "What are you doing? How are you going to hear?" I said, "I'll hang the speaker on my ear, what do you think? Give me the ticket." They finally let me in. I ran to the refreshment stand to get a pizza box. However, the girls back at the party had called ahead and said, "Don't give out your pizza boxes tonight." So they wouldn't let me have one. But we had to have one to win. So I thought, "Somewhere in this place there's got to be a pizza box." What do you do with the box when you order pizza at a drive-in? A lot of people toss it out the window. So I knew someplace there was a pizza box. I ran up and down the rows until finally I spotted one. I was so excited to get it that I tripped over some speaker cables as I ran. Down I went. The box was right next to a convertible with four young women inside. They saw me running toward them and must have thought I was going to jump in. Suddenly they were all screaming at the top of their lungs. I didn't have time to explain—I just grabbed the pizza box and took off. A man parked two places down saw me running with the box, heard them screaming, and thought I had stolen their pizza. He threw the speaker out of the car and rumbled after me—he was chasing me in his car! I barely got out of there with my life. I jumped in our car, and we popped the next balloon. "Eek!" and away we went.

That whole night was like that. We roared around all over Salt Lake City doing crazy things. Finally, as it got near the end of the night, one of the last things we had to do was go up to the local "passion flats" where a few of the kids park on Saturday night. It was well-inhabited when we arrived. We got out of the car, and each of us tip-toed around knocking on the foggy windows of the parked cars, then handing in a pamphlet and running away. Of course, the pamphlets were entitled, "Why Stay Morally Clean?"

It had been a great night. Nobody had sneaked off to a corner to neck; none of us felt guilty about anything we had done. I went home and told my parents everything (almost) we had done.

We had so much fun that we decided we had better pay the girls back. The only problem was that we didn't have any money, so it would have to be a cheap date. Two weeks went by as we planned for the next group outing. We had a friend whose father owned a furniture company. We filled his big furniture truck with folding chairs. When everyone arrived, we all piled into the back of the truck, all fifty of us. Then we went on the cheapest date I've ever been on in my life! We found a drive-in theater that charged three dollars for every vehicle that drove in. They couldn't do anything but let us in, so in we went. They had us park on the back row because of the size of the truck. We got out all our chairs and put them down on the whole row by the speakers. We had big theater bags of popcorn and passed them out to everybody and just had a great time. It was so much fun and so inexpensive: six cents for a movie—not too bad! We decided we'd try it again a couple of weeks later. This time, though, we asked everybody to bring something more comfortable than folding chairs to sit on. The kids were carrying their recliners out and shoving them in the back of the truck. One kid brought a big package under his arm; he wouldn't tell us what it was. When we got to the drive-in, he opened his package. It was a hammock, and he stretched it out between two speaker poles. "I'm going to listen in *stereo,*" he said.

The whole crazy summer was like that. It was great to get to know so many more people. It was one of the best summers I ever had because of following that principle taught by Elder Kimball. When September came and it was time to go back to school, I registered as a *senior.* Oh, it's nice to be a senior. You walk in and say, "Hi, everybody, it sure is nice to be with me!" I went in to pick up my registration packet, so I could sign up for my classes, when in came Steven, a friend of mine. I noticed that he had a pink slip in the back of his registration packet. "What's that for?" I asked. He said, "I'm checking out of school. I've got to support my family." I said, "Did something happen to your parents or something?"

13

He said, "No, it's not my parents. This is *my* family. Becky and I have been married for a couple of weeks, and we're going to have a baby in about six months. I've just got to be able to support my family."

Well, we had a really good talk, and I had a sad realization. Steve and Becky were sitting behind me at the fireside when an apostle of the Lord stood before us and said, "Don't stay out late alone; don't do these things. Stay in a group." They had rejected the words of a man we sustained as a prophet. They had been invited to the first group party, but they didn't come. Do you know why? They didn't think they could have any fun with a group. They didn't think an eighty-year-old man could tell them anything. They followed the light of their own conceit and said, "No, I'm going to do what *I* think is right." They wouldn't listen to the counsel of a prophet. And because they wouldn't, they left school for the last time. They have had many struggles since. The pain and sorrow that have come to that couple could have been changed if they had really listened when they sat at a fireside at the feet of one they sustained as a prophet. Instead, they said, "No, I will *not* follow your advice."

I know by direct experience how much our prophets love the youth, and that as we follow a prophet we can be happy. One day I was walking out of the Church Office Building parking lot, and there stood the prophet. I walked over and said, "President, may I talk to you for just a minute?" He put his arm around me, and as we were walking along together, I said, "President, I know that there have been times lately when you've received some criticism. However, I want to tell you that I've been with the youth of the Church, and I know they love you. I've seen youth who delight in following your counsel." He stopped in the middle of the parking lot, and he turned around and looked into my eyes. Then he said, "Would you do something for me?" "Anything," I said. "The next time you're with the youth, would you tell them how much I love them? For forty-two years I've never forgotten them in my prayers. The youth of the Church are the hope of the future. They are so important that I hear the apostles pray for them every week, and we never forget the youth." He bore his testimony to me about who you are. Then he stopped and said, "What I really wish they knew is how much the Lord loves them. I know the Lord loves the youth."

When I was leaving on my mission, many of the missionaries were called over to the temple for a meeting. To me, this was a very sacred experience. President Lee came in to talk to us. He announced, "Elders, I have two hours. If you have any questions at all, I'd be glad to answer them. What would you like to know?" Everyone asked questions of President Harold B. Lee. Finally one young elder stood up in the back and said, "President Lee, I came to this room up a spiral staircase. I was reading Church history the other day, and I read that on one of the stairwells of the temple, the Savior appeared to one of the presidents of the Church. Could you tell me which stairwell it is? I'd just like to know where He was." Then the missionary sat down. It was a simple question, really. President Lee looked down quietly for a long time. Then he looked up and said, "Elder, I think what you're asking me is, 'Where has the Lord been in the temple?' Is that what you'd like to know?" The elder nodded his head. President Lee then explained, "I hope this doesn't surprise you, but this is the Lord's house. He frequents these halls often. In fact, he might even be with us today."

We say there's a prophet on the earth. That means he really is a prophet. He receives instruction and guidance from our Elder Brother and Our Heavenly Father. They are at the head of this Church.

President Kimball walked into the funeral of President David O. McKay. A religious leader from another faith, a friend of President Kimball, had come to pay his respects. As he shook hands with President Kimball, he said, "I'm so sorry the head of your Church died." President Kimball said, "I am too. But isn't it wonderful that He rose on the third day?" If

15

there's anybody who knows the truth of what I'm talking about, it is our living Prophet, for whom the fog is lifted. I know that as we follow him, great joy comes and great joy will follow. That doesn't mean that our lives will be without trials, but it does mean that we will be prepared for what is ahead. I hope that this simple example might be generalized into many areas of our lives. I feel deeply that this generation will be ready to fulfill their divine destiny only by learning to follow the living Prophet with a greater exactness than possibly any generation has done before. The fog in our lives can become thick, and we need to rely on our ability to develop faith in one for whom the fog has lifted. It is my prayer that we can do this in a more complete way than any other generation in history.

Scott Anderson is an institute teacher at Utah Valley Community College in Orem, Utah. He enjoys construction work, sports, writing, and singing, and he has traveled to Egypt, Israel, Greece, Germany, and many other places. He and his wife, Angelle, have six children.

16

Chapter 2

Rad, Hot, Cool, and Awesome—
Do Spirituality and Popularity Mix?

Randall C. Bird

For as long as I can remember, I have wanted to be a professional football player. I have dreamed of playing cornerback for the Los Angeles Rams. At a very young age, I started working to develop myself physically so that I could play. I had a successful high-school football career and went on to play college ball in hopes of realizing my dream.

In college football, the coaches had us do some really strange drills. They called one drill the figure eight. In this drill, the defensive backs (of which I was one) would line up back to back with the All-American fullbacks (230 pounds of beef) and then run in a semi-circle ending up heading straight toward each other. This naturally resulted in a collision that was usually quite painful for me. The coaches said they were making us "tough."

The next drill we did involved boxing. The coaches would invite a small defensive back to kneel down and put on a pair of boxing gloves. Then they would invite our All-American lineman, weighing 260 pounds, to kneel down across from the defensive back and put on a matching set of gloves. Upon hearing the coach's whistle, the two team members were to hit each other repeatedly for one minute. Once again, we were being made "tough."

Following these drills, the coaches had us run a mile in full gear in under six minutes. If we couldn't do it, we were to run it again. Again, we were being made "tough." In spite of what the coaches said, there were many times during the football practice when I felt that rather than being made tough, I was being made dead.

Looking back, I realize that the coaches really were trying to toughen us up, not just put us through agony. They knew that to make it in football, a player has to be physically strong. Life is a lot like that. However, being physically tough isn't what is needed in today's world—we need to be spiritually tough. Being spiritually tough means being strong enough to do what you feel is the right thing. The problem is that just as I wondered about my coaches' efforts to make me physically tough, many young people today worry about being spiritually tough. They are afraid that if they are spiritually tough, they won't be popular.

An experience I had in high school haunts me to this day because I didn't do the right thing. Instead, I followed the crowd—I did the popular thing.

There was a girl in our high school who was not beautiful by the world's standards. To make things worse, a group of young men decided to give her a nickname and poke fun at her. They called her the "Foo." Every time the "Foo" came through the doors of the school, this group of boys, seated on the heaters in the hall, would yell, "Oooh! It's the Foo." Then they would run down the hall to get away. Then, I guess to add excitement to the game, the "Foo" would chase after them.

The girls at our school were embarrassed and sad that the boys were involved in such a thing. They would frequently say, "You guys make us sick." The boys would answer, "Yeah, that's us."

Eventually, the game got even worse. The boys said, "If the 'Foo' ever touches you, you have to marry her." I can still remember one day when the "Foo" was chasing a group of boys around the corner and they came running directly toward my locker. A great fear came over me that the "Foo" might touch me. Then I would have to marry her!

Such a thought should never have entered my mind, but it did. The next thing I knew, I found myself running from the "Foo" in hopes that she wouldn't touch me and I wouldn't have to marry her. She stopped in front of my best friend's locker. Russ should have known that he couldn't hide from the "Foo" in a locker, but he tried anyway. So there stood Russ with his arms and legs sticking out of the half-closed locker and the "Foo" in front of it. She yanked open the door. The look on Russ's face resembled something from a horror film, and he yelled as the "Foo" touched him. That night when Russ came to football practice, many of the team members offered him the openers from pop cans as imitation wedding rings to pick from so he could marry the "Foo."

The game continued as the Lettermen's Club decided to nominate the "Foo" for homecoming queen. The contestants would wear their formal dresses and appear before the entire student body. They would answer questions and do a poise and appearance routine before the voting took place.

The day arrived when each of the contestants was to go through this ordeal. I was asked to open the curtains for each contestant. As the "Foo" came on stage, she seemed almost humorous. Her dress was out of style, and her hair was a bit messy. Her make-up looked more like that of a clown than of a queen contestant. She went through her routine to the cheers of most of the boys in the student body, who yelled, "Vote for the 'Foo.' "

As I closed the curtain at the end of her performance, she walked toward me, then stopped about a yard away. Her head dropped, and she started to cry. For the first time, I realized that the "Foo" had feelings. Then came the hardest thing I've ever done—I asked the "Foo" for forgiveness. She shook her head and said, "Oh, it's okay. I understand."

That night at football practice, the word was out that I had asked the "Foo" for forgiveness. As each of the ball players walked by me, they stumbled and landed on me clumsily, saying, "Oh, will you please forgive me?" I couldn't wait to get them out on the practice field so I could teach them a lesson. You see, this group of boys had led me to believe that it wasn't popular to treat people kindly if they were different from the rest of us. I was misled.

While teaching young people, I've often asked, "Do you feel that girls are more spiritual than boys?" I've always been amazed that most people answer yes to that question. But I can see a couple of reasons why we might feel that way. First, girls generally express their spiritual feelings more openly and emotionally than boys do. It's normal during a testimony meeting for an entire room of girls to be in tears. It's almost like girls look around the room to find someone crying and then say, "Oh, look, there's someone in tears. Let's join in." We need to be careful not to mistake tears for the Spirit. An emotion can accompany the Spirit, but tears alone are not a sign of the Spirit. We look around to to see who's crying and then think that they are the ones who are spiritual. That isn't always the case.

Another reason we may feel that girls are more spiritual than boys is because of the way boys sometimes act. For example, some boys seem to get a thrill out of causing Sunday School teachers to resign. I get the impression that some boys keep a huge chart on the wall of their bedroom with check marks for each teacher they've driven out. It is not uncommon for a teacher to be enthusiastically reaching a key point in a lesson only to hear a strange sound coming from a young man in the room. Why do guys do things like that? Girls frequently attribute it to their lack of spirituality. However, I find it hard to believe that a young man who is supposedly spiritually dead during his high-school years can be transformed in a matter of three short months following graduation into a spiritual giant who is serving the Lord on a mission.

I tend to believe that young men and many young women feel that it's not popular to be good. So instead of allowing their true spiritual strength to show, they hide it behind silly

20

remarks and actions or an apathetic attitude toward anything spiritual.

I had a young man in my seminary class who, every time I marked reading charts, would say that he hadn't read further than 1 Nephi in the Book of Mormon. This young man was a state champion wrestler and was very popular with his peers. At the close of the year, he came up to me and said, "Brother Bird, I just thought you'd like to know that I've finished the Book of Mormon." After I picked myself up off the floor, I asked, "Why didn't you tell me sooner?" He replied, "I didn't want people to think I was spiritual."

Our society has apparently been somewhat successful in convincing people that being good is not popular. Young people are afraid of being labeled "Molly Mormon" or "Peter Priesthood." Instead of living up to their spiritual potential, they hide their light under a basket in the hope of being more popular.

Too many of us feel that what we wear, what we drive, or the group we hang around with is what makes us popular. This young man thought he couldn't read the Book of Mormon and be popular. I thought that being unkind to a girl who didn't quite fit our mold would make me more popular. In the long run, none of these things really matter. What matters is what we are inside—our spiritual strength—that enables us to feel good about ourselves. When we feel good about ourselves, then others feel good around us.

Several years ago I taught a young man who was this kind of person. Rich had been voted the A-2 player of the year in Idaho. He stood about 6'4" tall and weighed about 220 pounds. The guy was built—his body looked like an upside-down pyramid. The girls all thought he was handsome, but his physical traits aren't what impressed me. He was tough spiritually.

At one time in his school, it was popular to throw the girls into the boys' locker room in the hopes of embarrassing them. One day Rich happened to be in the dressing room when this happened. As the girl was thrown screaming into the locker room, Rich, who was totally dressed, left. He walked toward a group of young men who were laughing at the incident. Rich asked if any of them had thrown the girl in, and one young man responded, "Yes, I did." Rich grabbed the young man by the shirt, lifted him up against the wall, and asked, "Did you think it was funny?"

Meanwhile, the girl had left the locker room and was watching from a distance. The boy hanging from Rich's hand shook his head until his cheeks flapped, and with fear in his voice he replied, "No, no."

Then Rich said something that perhaps was not very Christian. He said, "If you ever do that again, I'll break your face!" Then he put the boy back down.

Now here is an important question: Do you think Rich became any less popular because he refused to go along with something he felt was wrong, even though it was considered the popular thing to do? Of course he didn't. In fact, you can probably imagine what was going through the mind of the girl who watched from a distance. You can almost hear her thinking, "Oh, what a man!"

Rich's spiritual strength didn't stop with this incident. Once we were playing a key football game between the first and second teams in the state. Following a sound defeat (the score was 41-6), this young man stepped onto the bus to find members of his team swearing and being downright crude. Rich stood up and said, "Now, we got beat, but we're not that kind of a team, so knock it off." Silence replaced vulgarity. What an example he was to the rest of the team.

You may be thinking, "Sure, he can get away with that. After all, he was 6'4" and weighed 220 pounds. What if he'd have been 5'4" and weighed 110?" Actually, I don't think that would have mattered much to Rich. I can almost picture him standing with his tiny frame and yelling in his high-pitched voice, "Now you guys sit down or I'll hit you in the knee."

You see, it wasn't Rich's size, or his good looks, or his

athletic abilities that made him what he was. There are plenty of big, good-looking athletes who don't have the spiritual strength to stand up for what is right. It took courage for Rich to live up to his standards just as it does for someone who isn't quite as physically gifted. Standards should always remain the same regardless of size.

Rich isn't the only young person I've seen who is spiritually tough. I once had a seminary class president who felt that as many senior girls as possible should attend the senior ball. Some boys sat back and poked fun at the girls who didn't have dates, but not this young man. He privately asked each girl in his class if she had a date or not. These girls were not too proud to say no if they didn't. Then he found out which of the boys didn't have dates and let them know which of the girls were still available. By the time the prom came along, most of those girls had dates.

I've seen other young men setting great examples and magnifying their priesthood. I remember a time near the end of a school year when I was teaching a class of all seniors. They were some of the finest people I knew, and they were popular, too. The only problem was that they hadn't really jelled as a class. The unity just wasn't there.

I felt prompted to have a time the last week of school when they could share their feelings, experiences, and testimonies with each other. I stood up, told the class what I had planned, and then sat back down, praying that someone would stand up.

The first person to come to the front of the class and sit on my desk was a boy. Now, that isn't usually what happens—usually a girl gets up first and then lots of girls follow her. But this young man sat in front of the class and shared some special experiences from his life. He mentioned that once while playing varsity basketball, he was undercut while going for a lay-up. When he came down, he fell on the floor, which caused severe injuries. Then the ambulance took him to the hospital. The best part of his testimony was when he said,

"What most of you don't know is that I died on the way to the hospital. And I'm so grateful to my dad, who holds the priesthood, for giving me a blessing and saving my life."

He wept as he shared this experience with us. Needless to say, you can imagine what all the girls were doing—they were breaking out the handkerchiefs, life preservers, rubber rafts, and so on.

When this young man sat down, a choice young woman who sat across the room turned in her seat, faced him, and said, "You're neat." Now, I hadn't seen that happen for a long time, and it brought a special spirit into our classroom.

Immediately after she said that, another young man stood and bore his testimony. Maybe he wanted the young woman to say that he was neat, too. As a matter of fact, almost five or six boys bore their testimonies before the girls could get up to the front. It was one of my greatest experiences.

The bell rang before all the students had finished bearing their testimonies. Not a soul moved. The class president, a rather tall, dark, handsome, and strong young man, stood and said, "Brother Bird, we're not leaving until we hear from the rest of the class." I said they would be marked for cutting their next class, and I also mentioned that I had another class coming in.

"Put your other class in another room," he said, and since he was much larger than I, I did what he asked me. The class continued their special experience together and then stood to go back to the high school for their government class.

Now as they sat in goverment class, a strange thing happened. The boys felt they had to change their emotions because it wasn't cool for a guy to cry in government. Only when grades come out is it all right for a guy to cry in government. As sometimes happens, two girls looked at each other and said, "Wasn't that neat what we had in seminary today?" The emotions of the previous hour returned, and the girls started to cry. Other girls in the class also joined in, making it a community affair. The guys responded by yelling,

"You girls knock it off." That was their way of saying, "We're just about ready to start crying too, so you had better quit." Their attitude didn't mean they weren't as spiritual as the girls. Rather, it meant that they didn't want to show their emotions through tears—especially in government class.

I've always noticed that following a tear-jerker of a movie, I'll hear a deep voice say, "Brother Bird, you'd better leave the lights off for a few minutes so these girls can put their faces back on." What the young man is really saying is, "I've got some tears that I still have to put back in my eyes, so please don't turn on the lights or you'll embarrass me."

Young men have just as strong testimonies as do the young women of the Church. Please don't be embarrassed to do what's right. As a matter, of fact, it's kind of nice to see a boy cry when Bambi's mother gets shot. Of course, I understand that it is a bit embarrassing if you're crying and you look over to find out that your date isn't.

I've told you about several young men who were spiritually tough, but that doesn't mean they were the only tough ones. I've known a lot of spiritually tough young women too.

A girl at our high school had just received the most votes in the primary election to be cheerleader for the next school year. Following the announcement, she came over to the seminary building and asked if she could use my office for a few minutes. "Of course," I said.

About fifteen minutes later, she came out of the office, and I could tell that it had been an emotional experience for her. She said, "I guess the Lord doesn't want me to be a cheerleader next year."

I sat in shock as she returned to the high school and removed her name from the ballot. The next day, I asked her why she had withdrawn her name, and she replied, "I just feel that the Lord has something else for me to do." Less than a week later, the stake president called her to his office and issued a call from the Lord to serve as president of the entire seminary.

The following year, I had a similar experience. Another girl had just received the most votes in the primary election for cheerleader and came over to the seminary. She also asked to use my office. "Oh, no, here we go again," I thought. Sure enough, the young woman came out and announced that she was not going to continue with the election. She withdrew her name from the ballot.

Now, if you are a cheerleader, don't panic. It is perfectly fine to try out for extracurricular activities. What I am trying to show is what happened in the lives of these two young women who followed the promptings of the Spirit in spite of what was popular in the eyes of their peers. They followed what the Lord had in store for them. They were being spiritually tough.

The second girl later told me that she felt impressed to quit the election because she wanted to spend more time with her mother. She felt that when she came home, her mother left; and that when her mother came home, she left. Her life with her mother had been a revolving door with no one ever getting off.

That fall when school began again, I saw this young woman for the first time since school had ended the year before. She told me that her mother had been diagnosed as having leukemia and had only three months to live.

Almost three months later, I attended the funeral of this girl's mother. As I approached this valiant daughter of our Father in heaven, she hugged me and said how special it had been for the Lord to allow her this time with her mother before she left this life.

You are part of a chosen generation. What a thrill it is to see young people following the promptings of the Spirit. How wonderful it is to see them becoming spiritually tough. It may not always be easy for you to be spiritually tough. At times, doing the right thing may not seem like the popular thing to do. But if you will, you will gain the admiration of classmates, peers, parents, and leaders, and, more important, the approval of our Father in heaven. May the Lord continue to inspire you to make good choices, and may you have the courage to follow that inspiration.

Randall C. Bird is the regional coordinator for seminaries in the Shelley, Idaho, area. He and his wife, Carla, have six children. Randall enjoys sports and has coached high-school football. In high school, he was named to the Idaho all-state teams in football and track.

Chapter 3

What Are You Carrying in Your Backpack?

John G. Bytheway

"I can't go another step!" The words echoed loudly through the trees, and we all turned around to see who said them. I guess someone was finally willing to admit that the hike was anything but fun. He was sick and would pass out at any moment if we didn't stop.

The Scoutmaster decided to take him back down the trail and drive him home. He told us to keep going and that he would catch up with us as soon as he could. The fun of having a new blue-light special K-Mart backpack had long since passed, and I wondered how much longer it would be before we'd arrive at the lake. It wasn't that bad at first. The trail was straight and smooth and easy. But after about an hour of walking, we got to the point where there was nowhere to go but up, and the trail became increasingly rocky and difficult.

The Scoutmaster asked me to assume command (I was the ranking Senior Patrol Leader—what we call SPL in official Scouting circles), and we continued our death march up Mount Everest. We continued, right foot, left foot, right, left, slowly making progress.

Another half-hour had not gone by when another Scout complained in almost the same words: "I can't go another step." I guess it was contagious.

It was time for a troop meeting. The eight of us remaining decided the only way we could beat the mountain was if we took it on a little bit at a time. We'd take a hundred steps, then rest for a minute, then take another hundred, then rest for a minute, and so on. What a dumb idea. It takes a long time to go five miles a hundred baby steps at a time. It was like playing "Mother May I" for three hours. Why couldn't the Forest Service just install escalators?

We trudged on. The sun set, and it began to get dark. I remember using the flashlights around me to help light my way. We'd hike, then we'd rest, then we'd hike, then we'd rest. The trail was rocky and steep, and we all began to wonder, "Is this the right trail? Where's the lake? Maybe we're lost."

Another couple of hours went by, and I remember coming across something very strange. I saw stars, but they were on the ground. Not being real intelligent, I just stared at them for a minute trying to figure out what was going on. Finally a ripple rolled through the stars, and I realized I was standing a foot away from the shallow northern bay of the lake! I had almost led my Scout troop right into the water. Can you imagine the headlines? "Eight Scouts Drown While Trying to Build Fire Underwater—Investigators Wonder: Were They Brain Dead or Teenage Mutants?"

As we started to unload our packs, we quickly learned why our tired Scout had had such a hard time. He opened up his flap, and the first thing he took out was a large can of Dinty Moore beef chunk stew. He set it down, and we felt the earth shake as it hit the ground. Then he took out an industrial-size can of Nalley's chili con carne, and another can of Dinty Moore beef chunk stew, made to serve about forty-five people. The rest of the troop were standing together in awe as this Scout unloaded his personal two-year food-storage program in the dirt. He had also packed three different flashlights (each with heavy batteries) and three canteens full of water, not to mention the essentials like tent and sleeping bag.

Backpacking is hard. Tom loaded his pack with many

items that were too heavy, that he didn't need, that weighed him down and made the hike a lot harder than it needed to be.

Life is often hard. Each morning we face the mirror and begin to load up. We toss in heavy, unnecessary baggage, worthless things that are good for nothing—like bricks and rocks and tree stumps. We say to ourselves, "My nose is too big, my hair's too thin," or "I'm not popular—people don't like me." We tell ourselves we're unworthy or unlovable. Then we ask why life has to be so difficult as we drag this worthless cargo of junk off to school. The trail is rough—we cannot change the trail. But we can make the hike so much easier if we will *change what's in our pack*. What are you carrying in *your* backpack?

Let me suggest three things to help us find the rocks and bricks in our packs and throw them out! The first is simply to understand who we are. This is nothing new. We sing songs about it, we read scriptures about it, we talk about it in seminary. But we must, at some time, understand what it really means.

When I was on my mission in the Philippines, my companion and I were given a referral. The man's name was Johnny Sajonas. We were told that he was about seventy-five and was frustrated with religion. He couldn't find the answers and was bordering on atheism. We approached his home and knocked on the post of his fence just outside the door. A partially bearded old man with a cane in his hand and a frown on his face appeared. He asked what we wanted. We told him that we were missionaries from The Church of Jesus Christ of Latter-day Saints and that we wanted to share a message with him about the Lord.

He stood silently, examining us from head to foot for a moment, and then said, "You're very young. I doubt you can teach me anything." I was a bit surprised, but I smiled and responded, "Oh, sir, we have great confidence in our message. Please let us come back and share it with you." He took a minute to think about it and finally mumbled, without changing his tone or his expression in the least, "You come back tomorrow at ten o'clock." Then he turned and walked into the house.

The next day when we arrived at Brother Sajonas's house, he invited us inside and we sat down on a bamboo bench in front of his Nestle's Quick table (that's what we call a coffee table in the Church). We started out, as was customary at that time, with the discussion on the Restoration of the Church. As Elder Warren began to teach, we noticed that our investigator was rather anxious and fidgity. He'd look at the floor, then at the ceiling, then off to the side. You had to be a gymnast to keep eye contact! And he didn't seem to be listening to what we were saying.

After a few moments, he interrupted us in mid-sentence, looked straight at me, and asked in an angry tone, "Who created evil?" We sat there for a moment in shock. Then I cleared my throat and responded like any good senior companion, "Well . . . uh . . . you see, it's uh . . . uh . . . Elder Warren, you wanna take that one?" Just then, I understood his *real* question—did *God* create evil. I picked up my Bible and said, "Sir, it has to do with a place called the pre-mortal existence," and I began to explain. I doubt he'd ever heard anything like it before, since the belief in a pre-earth life is rather unique to our church. I referred to the book of Isaiah and told him about Lucifer, the son of the morning, who, by his own choice, rebelled against God and fell from heaven, becoming the father of lies and the father of evil. Our investigator just sat for a second, then nodded slowly as if to say, "Okay . . . I'll buy that for now." I hoped I had answered him correctly, and I felt relieved that he was satisfied with our response.

We tried to continue where we left off in the Restoration discussion, but again our investigator was off in another world. He stopped us in mid-sentence again and loudly demanded, "Why are there so many wars?" "Uh . . . well, you

31

see, it's uh . . . uh . . . Elder Warren, you wanna . . . " The answer came again, "You see, sir, it has to do with something we received in the pre-mortal existence. It's called free agency." I explained how people have a hard time getting along with one another, and that this was true about the leaders of our countries as well. Sometimes we don't do a very good job of running this world, and we get in fights and in wars. But if God came down and solved all our problems, we wouldn't be able to learn and grow, and that's what life is for. This answer seemed to get him thinking, and we continued with our discussion.

He waited a minute and then stopped us a third time and asked, "Why do so many children starve?" What a good question! Elder Warren and I had seen things in the Philippines that we'd never seen before. Malnutrition and poverty were almost everywhere we looked. Little kids, really little, some not even old enough to walk, would crawl and play around open sewers. Some would get parasites that would stunt their growth. Others had patchy rashes on their heads that would make their hair fall out. Some had open cuts and wounds that weren't properly cleaned and dressed and never seemed to heal. I had asked myself the same question. I had heard it explained once in Sunday School, and I tried to explain it to Brother Sajonas. "Heavenly Father has a different perspective than we do. When we see a child die, that's how we see it— a child dying. Heavenly Father, on the other hand, sees one of his own spirit children being set free and coming home to him after being away for only a short time."

It was at this point I had one of those "Aha!" experiences. It dawned on us that we were teaching the wrong lesson. For every question he asked, the answer came from the plan of salvation. We should have been teaching the Purpose of Life discussion! The introductory visual aid for that discussion listed three questions. I turned to it and began to explain. A change of expression came over his face, and I watched him in silence as he read and reread each question:

Where did I come from?

Why am I here?

Where will I go when I die?

His eyes moistened, and tears fell from his face. I had never had this reaction with this picture or any other in my flip chart, and I didn't know what was going on. I looked at the picture myself to make sure Elder Warren hadn't stuck a picture of me in there. I looked at Elder Warren and looked back at Brother Sajonas, and just then the Spirit said, "Elder, testify." I sat up on the edge of the bench, looked in Brother Sajonas's eyes, and testified to him that we knew where we came from, why we were here, and where we were going. He sat silent for a moment. Then he stood up, motioned for us to wait, and walked slowly into the back of the room. He picked a little red book from the shelf and made his way back to where we were sitting. Then he opened up the book to the back inside cover, held it up in front of my face, and said tearfully, "You are so young!" He had written some things on the back inside cover. In his shaky old handwriting, it said:

My Eternal Questions

1. Where did I come from?
2. Why am I here?
3. What do I need to accomplish?
4. Where will I go when I die?

After I read the words, I looked up into this sweet old man's tear-filled eyes as he said, "You are so young. And you've come from so far to teach me these things."

The next day we laid the entire plan of salvation out on the table for him with cardboard visual aids. I remember watching Brother Sajonas bow his head, cover his face with his hands, and sob, "I have been looking for this for forty years." This sweet old man, an educated man, wanted so desperately to know who he was, where he was from, and what God expected him to do. And a couple of nineteen-year-olds walked in and told him all about it.

You are so young. And yet you know where you come

33

from, why you're here, and where you're going. Why do you know? Why have you been given the privilege when there are millions, perhaps billions of people in this world who don't know? Many of them are miserable and frustrated like Brother Sajonas, who are "only kept from the truth because they know not where to find it." (D&C 123:12.)

Perhaps you have earned this privilege because of *who you are*. President Ezra Taft Benson, speaking to seminary and institute teachers said: "I am sure you appreciate the fact that you have been given custody of some of the choicest spirits of all time. I emphasize that. These are not just ordinary spirits, but among them are some of the choicest spirits that have come from heaven. These are they who were reserved to come forth in this time to bear off the kingdom triumphant." ("The Gospel Teacher and His Message," from *Charge to Religious Educators*, p. 48.)

I remember as a teenager sitting in firesides and hearing speaker after speaker say, "You're a child of God," and I thought, "Big deal, isn't everyone? Why should that make me feel so good?" What, then, does it mean to be a child of God? Why is it talked about so much? Being a child of God means that God is intensely interested in us and in our progress. He wants us back. His work is to bring to pass our immortality and eternal life. And there's more: Not only are you a child of God, but you are also a *valiant* child of God saved for the last days. You are the best of the best. Do you believe it? Someone who truly knows who he or she is would never think of doing things like drinking, taking drugs, or being immoral. I think every time our knees hit the floor, we should ask Heavenly Father to help us understand who we are.

Sometimes in this hike of life, we have to help each other a step at a time. A second step in lightening our load as we trudge onward and upward is to decide to be a "builder" instead of a "wrecker." Anyone can tear a building down—

all it takes is a big hammer. But it takes knowledge and skill to put up a building.

We can choose whether to be either a builder or a wrecker. We can sit in our Sunday School, MIA, or school classes and say, "boooorrrrring." Or we can say, "What can I do to make this a better class?" We have free agency. We can criticize, complain, and cut people down, or we can build, bolster, and brighten the lives of those around us.

A few years ago, I taught at a youth conference at San Diego State University. On the afternoon of the first Monday, the participants were coming into the cafeteria for lunch. Three young men, each about the size of a vending machine, entered the cafeteria. Once they had loaded their trays with food (and I mean loaded—they should've brought a U-Haul trailer), they turned and looked around the cafeteria for a place to sit. They could've sat just about anywhere they wanted because no one would dare complain, but they spotted a table in the back occupied by one young man who was barely old enough to attend the conference. The three of them turned and headed in that direction.

Now what would you think? Here are these three tough guys heading toward the table of a little kid. The counselors at the table thought the gruesome threesome were going to give this kid a bad time, and they were preparing to come to his defense. Imagine our surprise when one of these large young men, seventeen-year-old Jerry, put his hand on the shoulder of the boy at the table and politely asked if they could eat with him. The boy nodded his head that they could join him (as if he would have said no), and these three wonderful young men sat down, ate their lunch, and made friends with him. I believe that angels in the room were doing high-fives. (I don't know exactly how angels rejoice, maybe they just look down and exclaim, "Thou art cool," but I'm sure they were pleased.) I don't believe Jerry himself understood what a Christian thing he had just done. Why was he able to do that? What made him able to reach out when many of us

35

are too fearful to try? I believe it was because Jerry had worked on point number one—he knew who he was. He knew that he didn't have to talk only to the people who looked like him, or dressed like him, or who played the same sports that he did, or who could bench press a Toyota like him, but he could talk to anyone, be their friend, and bring them in. He knew that it was nice to be important, but more important to be nice. Jerry was a builder. President Spencer W. Kimball once said: "God does love us, and he watches over us, but it is usually through another person that he meets our needs. Therefore, it is vital that we serve each other in the kingdom."

Jerry was that "other person" Heavenly Father used to help meet the needs of another. There's a great scripture that talks about loving not only the people that love us, but even those who don't: "If ye love them which love you, what reward have ye? do not even publicans the same? and if ye salute your brethren only, what do ye more than others? do not even the publicans so? Be ye therefore perfect, even as your Father which is in heaven is perfect." (Matthew 5:46–48.)

Even the devil has friends. It's easy to love those who love us. The challenge is to love those who are hard to love. You will be amazed at how much lighter your own load will become when you seek to help others lighten their loads. Throughout your life, you will be given opportunities to decide whether you will build or destroy. At work, at school, in the family, even at church. Will we gossip or will we build? Will we notice the person walking next to the lockers at school with his head down and his hands in his pockets and say to ourselves, "He's a loser," or will we walk up and say, "Hi"? Will we look for things to complain about, or will we look for ways to help? Will we talk about the faults of our leaders, or will we sustain them in their callings? We are allowed to decide whether we will be a part of the solution to this world's problems, or whether we will be a part of the problem. We can be on the Lord's side, or we can be on the other side. It is up to us.

The third thing we can do to lighten our load is best explained by an experience I had once at a youth conference. Some young women had disappeared during an activity and failed to show up that night at the curfew hour. When they finally did return, we could tell that they had been drinking. One of the rules of the conference was that participants must follow the standards of the Church or they would be sent home.

I sat down with one of these young women at about one o'clock in the morning, and we began to talk. She was embarrassed about what had happened and kept her head down and her eyes on the floor. We talked for quite a while about her interests and background, and when I felt that she knew I wasn't going to give her a big lecture, I began to ask her some questions.

"Could I be your big brother for a minute?"

"Uh-huh."

"Aimee, do you want to be good?" (I think that's a great question because the seventh chapter of Moroni tells us that we all have the light of Christ and a tendency toward the right.)

"Yeah, I guess so."

"Aimee, do you pray?"

"No."

"When was the last time you prayed?"

"Well, I give opening prayers in seminary or I bless the food, but I don't mean anything by it."

"Why not?"

The next thing she said was the classic brick in the backpack that is *most common* among youth I've worked with. She said: "Well, I've made some mistakes, and I don't feel comfortable praying. I don't see why Heavenly Father would listen to me because I've done so many dumb things."

This belief is the most common but often the most difficult

of problems to overcome. Every time I've shared this story, I've had young people tell me that they've felt just like Aimee. Once Satan convinces us that there's no turning back, we may stop praying or reading our scriptures or doing the things that bring happiness and the Spirit of the Lord into our lives.

Often we don't understand that the times we feel least like praying are when we need to pray the most. We can come up with a million excuses, but none of them are very good. Saying that you don't want to pray because you feel unworthy is like saying that you don't want to see a doctor because you don't feel well.

Nephi said, "If ye would hearken unto the Spirit which teacheth a man to pray ye would know that ye must pray; for the evil spirit teacheth not a man to pray, but teacheth him that he must not pray." (2 Nephi 32:8.) If you've felt like you shouldn't pray, you've listened to the instructions of the wrong spirit! Heavenly Father always wants you to pray.

Prayer is a powerful tool for solving problems. Elder Thomas S. Monson once said: "Prayer can solve more problems, alleviate more suffering, prevent more transgression, and bring about greater peace and contentment in the human soul than can be obtained in any other way."

As uncomfortable as we may sometimes feel, as unworthy as we may feel, even when we know we've done wrong, we can be assured that there is someone who will always be there, and who will always be willing to listen.

Bishop H. Burke Peterson has said: "I want you to know that I know that whenever one of Heavenly Father's children kneels and talks to him, he listens. I know this as well as I know anything in this world—that Heavenly Father listens to every prayer from his children. I know our prayers ascend to heaven. No matter what we may have done wrong, he listens to us." ("Prayer—Try Again," *Ensign*, June 1981, p. 73.)

I spent a couple of hours trying to convince Aimee that although she felt uncomfortable, she needed to pray. Aimee did pray that night, a simple prayer, but it was a start. I remember feeling that Aimee had made quite a turnaround that night.

Later on I started having doubts and lacking faith. How could one prayer on one night change a life around — especially when this had been going on for months? The next morning Aimee went home, and we continued with the youth conference. More than six months passed, and I received a letter from Aimee. She wrote: "Hey, buddy, how are things going? Everything seems to be just fine with me. I have come to realize how important it is to obey the commandments. I have been praying and reading scriptures — my life has totally changed. I don't even hang around the so-called cool people that drink. It's not worth it — they are not true friends. Guess what, I got my patriarchal blessing. That also helps me to be good. It encourages me a lot. I now know that life isn't just one big party. I love ya! Aimee." Aimee learned to pray, and she and her Heavenly Father turned her life around.

We have learned that man is that he might have joy, and yet many of us seem to insist on keeping the rocks in our backpacks by refusing to partake of the love of God and the forgiveness that he offers to all.

If we are to lighten our load, we must understand who we are. We must understand the identity of those around us and build them up. And, as Aimee discovered, we must strive to be worthy.

Yes, life is hard, and the trail does not get much easier. We can make the hike easier by emptying our backpacks of self-defeating attitudes, by building and serving one another, and by praying and repenting of our sins and striving to keep our lives clean along the way.

Let the Light of the World help you lighten your load. When things get really heavy, and you're tired and weary, remember the tender words of the Savior: "Come unto me, all ye that labour and are heavy laden, and I will give you rest. Take my yoke upon you, and learn of me; for I am meek and lowly in heart: and ye shall find rest unto your souls. For my yoke is easy, and my burden is light." (Matthew 11:28.)

John G. Bytheway coordinates BYU Outreach Youth Conferences. He recently graduated from Brigham Young University in marketing. Now he spends his leisure time running, reading, playing the guitar, and eating Twix candy bars (caramel, not peanut butter).

Chapter 4

Surviving the Teen Scene

Jack R. Christianson

Not long ago, in the quiet and darkness of the early morning, I was awakened by the sound of a frightened four-year-old who wanted to get into bed with her mother and me. She whispered something softly about having a nightmare. Then, trying to obtain my approval of her actions, she cuddled up close to me. I told her I loved her, and then she threw me the clinching line that allowed her to stay the remainder of the night. She put her head on my chest, asked me to hold her, and said, "I'm glad you're my dad, Dad." I melted. She knew it. I was like putty in her hands, being molded into anything she desired. Her wish was my command. I slid my left arm under her head and pulled her close. She complained briefly that her feet were cold, so I wrapped my right leg over her feet. Lying on my side, and having donated my arm as a pillow and my leg as a blanket, I tried desperately to go back to sleep. It didn't work. Each time I moved, my daughter would cling to me like a vine to a tree. It wasn't long before I had only about ten inches of bed to sleep on, and my left arm was numb under her head. Finally, I had to move my arm and try to stay on the bed. The night was long and memorable.

Two weeks later, again enjoying the bliss of sleep, I was awakened by a sweet, soft voice and someone tapping me on the shoulder. As my eyes began to focus, I recognized my four-year-old. She was crying. She had dreamed there were spiders all over her room. They were on the doors, mirrors, and clothes. Again she wanted to get in bed with us. Before I could answer, she leaped over me and slithered under the sheets. What was I to do? I desperately needed to sleep, but spiders?

It didn't take long to make a decision. Without hesitation, she moved close and said, "Dad, please hold me like you did the last time." I quickly put one arm under her head, another around her waist, and a leg over both of hers. There, in the darkness, with a child in my arms, I caught a glimpse of heaven. For a brief moment, as love, devotion, and dedication filled my entire being, I began to feel how much our Father in heaven must love each of his children.

In her time of fear and insecurity, she had come to me, her father. She had sought safety in the arms of a loving parent. The words "all that my Father hath" came driving into my heart. I wanted to give her everything I had or ever would have because of her love for me.

It wasn't long before she turned sideways and placed the heel of her foot in my face. Once more I had but a few inches of bed for sleep, but it didn't seem to matter. She was safe.

Sleep fled, and a dim ray of light from a nightlight made its way through the hallway and onto the little face beside me. A glimpse of heaven. Nothing was more important for that moment. A feeling of love for her that was greater than the love of life swept through me. Is this what Father feels, I wondered, when we come to him in our hours of need and say, "Please hold me, bless me like you did before?" I began to understand why he desired only to be called Father.

Perhaps this love for a child was the same that caused the "heavens to weep" (see D&C 76:26) and the Lord to declare that "the worth of souls is great in the sight of God" (D&C 18:10).

Our father must weep, as we do, with the thought of losing one of his "little ones." Every single soul—not just a chosen few—is precious, and he loves us. We must return to our Father and be held in his arms as my daughter came and was held in mine.

We need to know the reality of God and the divinity of his Son Jesus Christ. We should build our testimonies of the truthfulness of the Book of Mormon and the mission of Joseph Smith and the importance of following living prophets. But aside from these basic truths, there are five other important items necessary to achieve eternal life and return to our Father.

First, we must learn never to fear failure. Unfortunately many people, and especially the young, are so afraid of failing that they never attempt to achieve their goals or live their dreams. They are so afraid their peers will disapprove that many an unfulfilled dream remains where it was given birth, in the mind. Certainly failure brings pain and is very difficult to handle. But there is nothing wrong with failure once in a while. I know of no one who has experienced any amount of success who has not also encountered a great amount of failure along the way. Of course, we should not obtain a Ph.D. in failure, but if we fear it, success in any area may elude us.

Because someone has done something wrong does not make him or her a bad person. Simply because people have failed at times does not prove they are failures. I wonder, from the eyes of the world, how many considered the life of Jesus Christ or Joseph Smith as failures? Each died as a young man for an unpopular cause. Their murders appeared to have stopped their work. How grateful we should be that they neither faltered nor feared to attempt to fulfill their missions. What if the fear of failure had held them back?

Perhaps one of the greatest and most often repeated stories in the Old Testament is that of David and Goliath. The story, found in 1 Samuel 17, unveils marvelous lessons in not fearing failure.

Goliath of Gath was the champion of the Philistines. He stood over nine feet tall. For forty days he taunted and disgraced Israel. Daily he asked for the Israelites to "give me a man, that we may fight together." (Verse 10.) David, the

43

youngest of eight sons, went to take food to his three eldest brothers, who served under Saul and witnessed the daily mockery. When he arrived near the battle zone, he heard the defiant Goliath. He saw the men of Israel run with fear from the giant's loathsome speech and threats. David asked the trembling men, "Who is this uncircumcised Philistine, that he should defy the armies of the living God?" (Verse 26.) David could hardly believe that all of Israel's army feared to fight the Philistine. He was met by a rebuke from his eldest brother, who scolded, "I know thy pride, and the naughtiness of thine heart; for thou art come down that thou mightest see the battle." (Verse 28.) David responded innocently but deeply, "What have I now done? Is there not a cause?" (Verse 29.)

Oh, what a question! Is there not a cause? If we have a cause, then why fear temporary failure? David must have resolved that the cause of the Master was worth risking failure against the giant.

David took the challenge, went to King Saul, and offered to fight the Philistine. Many must have laughed and mocked young David. But he did not fear. He did not use the king's armor but relied on his sling and stones and his faith in the God of Israel. He said, "The Lord that delivered me out of the paw of the lion, and out of the paw of the bear, he will deliver me out of the hand of this Philistine." (Verse 37.)

The scriptures tell the story: "And he took his staff in his hand, and chose him five smooth stones out of the brook, and put them in a shepherd's bag which he had, even in a scrip; and his sling was in his hand: and he drew near to the Philistine." (Verse 40.)

Why did David take five stones when he knew that one could accomplish the task? Could it be that young David realized the possibility of failure and prepared himself for it? Did he have the assurance that "if ye are prepared ye shall not fear?" (D&C 38:30.) David knew that he may not succeed in killing the giant on the first, second, or even third attempt.

David reached his goal because of his faith in God and himself. He did not fear failure but was prepared for it. He "hasted, and ran toward the army to meet the Philistine. And David put his hand in his bag, and took thence a stone, and slang it, and smote the Philistine in his forehead, that the stone sunk into his forehead; and he fell upon his face to the earth." (1 Samuel 17:48–49.) David knew that the outcome of his success was worth the risk of failing.

Second, we must learn never to fear truth, for only if we are unafraid of truth will we ever find it. Truth, if lived, may cause a person to change or admit that he or she is wrong. For many, leaving the comfort zone is very difficult. Those who live the truth have always been criticized. Christ was crucified and Joseph Smith was murdered for truth's sake. The Apostle Peter wrote, "There were false prophets also among the people, even as there shall be false teachers among you, who privily shall bring in damnable heresies, even denying the Lord that bought them, and bring upon themselves swift destruction. And many shall follow their pernicious ways; by reason of whom the way of truth shall be evil spoken of." (2 Peter 2:1–2.)

The pathway of truth is not always an easy one. It requires us to rid ourselves of the shackles of deception and see things as they really are and not as they may appear. The Lord told Joseph Smith, "Truth is knowledge of things as they are, and as they were, and as they are to come." (D&C 93:24.) Yet on the other hand, by living and finding truth, we obtain freedom. Jesus taught, "Ye shall know the truth, and the truth shall make you free." (John 8:32.) Unfortunately, often when young people live the truth and stand up to defend it, they may be thought of as weird or strange. It seems to be the norm to be good but not too good. Some young people think that if you are too good, then something must be wrong with you.

Some time ago I had an experience that drove home the need to never fear the truth in unforgettable fashion. I was a

45

speaker at a youth conference at a beautiful mountain resort nestled among the firs, pines, and ferns—a near-perfect setting for a youth conference.

For the evening session of the conference I was assigned to speak on the sensitive topic of music and how it affects us, a subject I had addressed many times previously.

As I was approaching the speaking arena earlier in the day, my stereo and briefcase in hand, I noticed four young men listening to some music. They saw me and immediately recognized me as someone different. I was dressed in a suit and tie and was carrying a stereo tape deck.

As I drew closer to them, the one holding the stereo set it down and started walking towards me. Though small in stature, he was very noticeable and appeared somewhat out of place at an LDS youth conference. His hair was unique. It was a conglomerate of styles. Hanging from his left ear was a cross earring. He wore a black leather jacket with a small chain hanging over one shoulder. Both wrists were covered with spiked wrist bands. His T-shirt had obviously been purchased at a concert he had attended—it bore the logo of the band that had performed.

As he came closer, I said hello and was met by an abrupt gesture that was so sudden I found it difficult to perceive if he were joking or if he were serious. Without any hesitation he poked me in the chest and blurted, "Are you the chump that's going to tell us all our rock 'n' roll music is bad and if we listen to heavy metal we're all going to hell?"

I was shocked. In disbelief I told him that I was the speaker and that I would share with him how to choose what music to listen to and how music affects our actions, feelings, thoughts, and spirituality, but that he would have to make his own decisions. Without waiting for more, he poked me in the chest a second time and asked basically the same question: Would he go to hell if he listened to heavy-metal music.

I responded by asking him to please refrain from poking me again. As the words were falling from my lips, his finger

46

was already on the way to my chest. "Listen," he said as the finger made contact a third time, "if you tell me my heavy-metal music or my rock 'n' roll is bad, I will get up and leave your discussion." In my mind, I reasoned if that was all it took, he was as good as gone. He walked away, somewhat jokingly saying, "I'll leave! I'll leave!"

Later on that evening, the time came to speak on music. When I reached the pulpit and looked at the audience, there he was, sitting on the second row, arms folded and eyes glaring the message, "Go ahead, try to teach me or make me change." I spoke for some time before I reached the point of teaching how to choose between what is "good" and what is "bad." I quoted some verses from the seventh chapter of Moroni. While doing so, some words from the film *Man's Search for Happiness* came racing into my mind: "Only if you are unafraid of truth will you ever find it." As I said the phrase, the words rang through the hall and into many hearts. I stopped, pointed at the young man, and repeated the phrase, insinuating that he was afraid of the truth and that it would elude him forever if he continued to fear it. I then asked the congregation some soul-searching questions. "Are you afraid of truth? Does it embarrass you that you are a member of the only true church of Jesus Christ and that you are supposed to live life differently than the rest of the world? Does it bother you to be identified with cleanliness, goodness, and virtue? Truth may require sacrifice, and it may be hard on the ego. Do you have the courage it takes to live truth?" Most in attendance, including me, were shocked with the straight-forwardness of my questioning.

While I was shaking hands afterward, the young man approached me, finger pointing but not touching. He asked to speak with me alone. We arranged a time for the following morning just before breakfast. He left. I went on shaking hands.

As I left the building and headed through the trees toward my sleeping quarters, I saw the young man standing behind a tree. My heart began pounding with anticipation as he approached me. His voice was soft and subdued. He asked if we could spend a few minutes talking before I retired. That few minutes turned into nearly three hours. After finding a place to sit and talk, I learned his name. He said he didn't want to wait until morning to talk because he might lose his courage by then. We talked. We cried. I learned.

He told me that for the first time in his life, he asked himself if he was afraid of the truth. He found that he was terrified. I asked why, and his threefold answer revealed a frightened but courageous young man. He said if he lived the truth, he would have to give up most of his friends because they were all involved in drugs and alcohol. I asked if he had been. He hung his head and wept as he told of his involvement.

Then he said if he lived the truth, he would have to get rid of all his music because it made him feel exactly the way he wanted to feel—angry. He explained his situation with his parents and how deeply he wanted to get back at one of them.

He went on to explain that if he lived the truth, he might have to go see his bishop. He explained some of his problems, and I assured him that he needed to go as soon as possible. He wanted to have the courage necessary to face and live truth, but he also realized the difficulty of change. He realized the necessity to sacrifice temporary pleasures for true eternal principles and peace.

As we sat talking and weeping together, both of us realized how difficult it is to live truth when so many are mocking and fearing it. We made some special promises to each other and then embraced. As I held this aching young man in my arms and listened to his sobs and pleadings for help to live truth, I determined that any price was worth paying in order to help him. He couldn't do it alone—he knew it and I felt it.

Much time has passed since that night in the forest. But I have never forgotten the pleading eyes and the quavering voice that asked so trustingly for help to live truth. To help ourselves and our loved ones return to our Father, we must never fear truth.

Third, we must learn to read the scriptures daily and "feast upon the words of Christ." (2 Nephi 32:3.) This is where much spiritual strength lies. In a time when so many people are struggling with life and when decisions seem so difficult to make, we can find comfort and hope in knowing that "angels speak by the power of the Holy Ghost; wherefore they speak the words of Christ. Wherefore, I said unto you, feast upon the words of Christ; for behold, the words of Christ will tell you all things what you should do." (2 Nephi 32:3.) The words of Christ will tell us not just some things but "all things" what we should do. How exciting! The answers to life's questions are found in the scriptures!

Could studying the scriptures be one of the major factors in overcoming the onslaughts and temptations of the adversary? Nephi answers that question with what he told Laman and Lemuel when they asked about the symbolism of their father's dream: They said to him, "What meaneth the rod of iron which our father saw, that led to the tree? And I said unto them that it was the word of God; and whoso would hearken unto the word of God, and would hold fast unto it, they would never perish; neither could the temptations and the fiery darts of the adversary overpower them unto blindness, to lead them away to destruction." (1 Nephi 15:23.) With this promise, how can we let a day go by without reading the scriptures? Something happens spiritually as we "treasure up in your minds continually the words of life." (D&C 84:85.) As we study the scriptures, we are able to see things more clearly, as they really are, and not simply as they appear.

By feasting upon the scriptures, we begin to become more effective in our prayers. In a revelation to Joseph Smith, Oliver Cowdery, and David Whitmer, the Lord said: "These words are not of men nor of man, but of me; wherefore, you shall testify they are of me and not of man; for it is my voice which speaketh them unto you; for they are given by my Spirit unto you, and by my power you can read them one to another; and save it were by my power you could not have them; wherefore, you can testify that you have heard my voice, and know my words." (D&C 18:34–36.)

The scriptures are one of the great keys to spiritual success, and somehow, some way, we must learn to love them. Learning to love the scriptures is no different from learning to love anything else. We must practice, practice, practice, and then practice some more. Never would we attempt to play in a major championship of any kind or play an instrument for a recital without having practiced for hundreds of hours. Yet many feel they can unlock the excitement and beauty of the scriptures by snacking on them for a few minutes a week. It doesn't work that way. Of course, snacking is better than starving, but the Lord reminds us that it is when we are "feasting" that the words on the page become a part of us and begin to be alive and exciting. Get to know the the scriptures, and your journey back to our Father will be a lighted one.

Fourth, I would also ask you to pray. Perhaps nothing else in this world can help us more than meaningful daily communication with our Father in Heaven. The Lord says, "The spirit shall be given unto you by the prayer of faith." (D&C 42:14.) When we have the Spirit, we then have another tool to see things clearly. President Joseph F. Smith taught that if we lose the Spirit by "crossing over the line of demarcation between the Lord's territory and Satan's territory, we do not think or reason properly." The Lord counseled the Prophet Joseph Smith to "pray always, that you may come off conquerer; yea that you may conquer Satan, and that you may escape the hands of the servants of Satan that do uphold his work." (D&C 10:5.)

Praying, like scripture study, takes practice. So often, it is easy to get discouraged and feel that the heavens are made of brass. However, as we learn the correct manner in which to call upon our Father, and as we obey the laws that govern the blessing of answers to prayers, miracles begin to happen. Isaiah taught us that if we fast properly, and prayer is part of fasting, "then shalt thou call, and the Lord shall answer; thou shalt cry, and he shall say, Here I am." (Isaiah 58:9.)

By learning to pray effectively and doing it regularly, we will not only "come off conquerer," but also the windows of heaven will be opened and our pathways lighted.

Some years ago during a terrible snowstorm, I was driving to a basketball game that didn't begin until 10:30 P.M. I had little desire to go but felt a prompting to attend. It was the first time I had ever felt prompted by the Spirit to go play ball. It seemed crazy, but nevertheless the feelings were strong. I didn't dare disobey. While waiting at a stoplight, I noticed a young man, who I assumed was a BYU student, struggling to cross the street. As I pulled through the light, I felt impressed to stop and help him. "How could I?" I thought. "I'll be late for the game." I pulled ahead, drawing closer to where he was crossing. He attempted to climb up on the snow-packed curb but couldn't.

Again I felt extremely impressed to stop and help him, but I didn't. I pulled through the light, rationalizing that he could make it on his own. Besides, I had to get to the ball game. At the next light I was feeling terrible. All the lessons on service and charity I had taught so many times were ringing in my ears. I felt so ashamed that I decided to go back and help him, even if it meant being late and possibly getting my car stuck in the snow while trying to turn around. When I reached the spot where the young man had tried to climb up on the curb, he was nowhere to be seen.

Somewhat frustrated, I pulled the car into the driveway of a parking lot and attempted to turn around. As I did so, the lights from the car swept across the snow, revealing someone lying on the ground. I immediately jumped from the car, yelling at the figure, asking if he was all right. To my surprise, he responded, "Paul, Paul, is that you Paul?" I had

51

no idea what he was talking about. I told him my name, then asked what in the world had happened.

He explained that he had been on his way home from work when he slipped on some ice or snow and broken his leg. He had crossed the parking lot, hoping to take a shortcut, when he slipped again. This time, however, he could not get up. He knew he could not be seen from the street, so he had begun to pray for help. After I carried him to my car, he explained that he knew his brother-in-law Paul was at home. He had prayed that the Lord would send Paul to get him. When I approached, he expected me to be Paul.

He thanked me graciously. I was numb with the thought of what might have happened had I not listened to the promptings of the Spirit. But even more important, what if he hadn't known how to pray? I don't believe he was an amateur. He knew the Lord would answer. He called, and the Lord answered; he cried, and the Lord said, "Here I am." The Lord didn't get Paul, for some unknown reason, but he answered the prayer with me! It wasn't much to work with, but the Lord got the job done. And if the Lord can answer the prayer of a humble young man in a snow-blanketed parking lot and use a rushing ball player to do it, he can certainly answer our prayers. Yes, we must get on our knees and pray.

The fifth and final aid in returning to our Father in heaven is to keep the Sabbath Day holy. I believe the Lord meant what he said in Doctrine and Covenants 59:9: "That thou mayest more fully keep thyself unspotted from the world, thou shalt go to the house of prayer and offer up thy sacraments upon my holy day." This again, is another key to seeing clearly and keeping away from the evil things of the world.

If we would never fear the truth, never fear failure, get into the scriptures, get onto our knees, and keep the Sabbath Day holy, we should then follow Nephi and "shake at the appearance of sin." (2 Nephi 4:31.) Then we would all return to the loving arms of our Father.

As a seven-year-old boy, Joseph Smith had to undergo a

terrible operation to remove a piece of infected bone from his leg. In those days, doctors did not know how to put someone to sleep during an operation, but they often offered liquor to help ease the pain. Young Joseph said, "I will not touch one particle of liquor, neither will I be tied down; but I will tell you what I will do. I will have my father sit on the bed and hold me in his arms, and then I will do whatever is necessary in order to have the bone taken out."

All Joseph wanted was to be held in his father's arms as my little daughter desired to be held in mine. All our Father desires is for each of us to return to his arms and to his love. May we incorporate these principles into our lives and help our loved ones do the same, and may we go to the Lord often with our plea: "Father, please hold me like you did last time."

Jack R. Christianson is the seminary principal at Springville High in Utah. He and his wife, Melanie, have four children. A popular youth speaker, he is the author of the book Music: Apples, or Onions. *He is a sports enthusiast (he especially likes skiing) and likes to read.*

Chapter 5

Diamonds or Zirconias?
You Choose

Vivian Cline

Several years ago there was a little doll called a "Cabbage Patch Kid." The doll was very expensive, and people would wait in line for hours just so they could buy one. The first time my husband and I saw the doll, we said to ourselves, "There is no way we will ever spend that much money for a doll that is so ugly." But we had a problem. Our problem was five years old. Her name was Audrey Sophia. From June of that year until December, Audrey reminded us every day that she wanted only two things for Christmas: a Cabbage Patch Kid and a Mickey Mouse phone. Every day, that's all I heard: "Mommy, don't forget to tell Santa Claus that I want a Cabbage Patch Kid and a Mickey Mouse phone. Remember, Mommy, a Cabbage Patch Kid and a Mickey Mouse phone. Mommy, did you write in my letter that I want a Cabbage Patch Kid and a Mickey Mouse phone?" So guess what Audrey got for Christmas? Right, a Cabbage Patch Kid and a Mickey Mouse phone.

I want you to know that as I wrote the check out for the doll, I suffered writer's cramp. I could not believe I was paying that much for such an ugly little doll! Why were these dolls so expensive? I found out that each doll came with its own set of adoption papers, so you didn't just buy them, you adopted them into your family. They also came with some of the strangest names I've ever heard. (We sent our papers back with a name change.) And each doll had a designer signature

54

on its little behind to prove its authenticity. This way the "parents" knew their doll was not a copy like many that began flooding the market. Most important of all, however, was that each of these dolls was considered an original, with no two exactly alike. That's why people were willing to pay so much money for them—each doll was unique.

Now there are other unique things in life besides Cabbage Patch dolls. I have something in mind that is rare, beautiful, unique, and much more expensive than dolls. Women sometimes refer to them as their best friends. Can you guess what that might be? If you guessed diamonds, you are exactly right.

Good diamonds are papered. Each has its own pedigree papers that tell all about that diamond: its carat weight, measurements, color, clarity, and flaws are all listed.

A few years ago, I was shopping at a local department store when suddenly a jewelry counter caught my eye. That's not terribly unusual for me, as I've always had a weakness for beautiful jewelry. Though I can't afford a lot of nice jewelry, I do enjoy wishing at the jewelry counters. As I was admiring the display of diamond rings, the clerk asked if I would like to try some on.

"No thank you," I said. "I couldn't possibly afford those beautiful rings."

"You can afford these rings," she said. "They are cubic zirconias, and they cost only $15.00." I was shocked! I had thought I had a good eye for expensive jewelry, but I could not tell the difference between those zirconias and real diamonds. I had been deceived by a cheap imitation.

In life, for everything of great value and lasting beauty, Satan has cleverly disguised a cheap imitation, something he would convince us would make us happy and bring us joy but in truth will not.

Think for a moment about diamonds in your life—things of greatest worth. How about the gospel, temple marriage, the scriptures, your family, your testimony and moral purity? All these do bring us joy and happiness. Think, for a moment, of some cubic zirconias in life—cheap imitations that Satan would have us believe bring joy and happiness. The television is loaded with them. All you have to do is turn on the tube, and they flash at you from all directions.

Drugs in particular have plagued our society for the past twenty years. Satan would have you believe that life is boring, that drugs will not only help you cope with life but also help you enjoy it. I never really understood how drugs work until a friend of mine, Paul Louden, who has worked for the Los Angeles Police Department as an undercover narcotics agent, explained it to me. He said that we all start out on a level of normality. When we take drugs, they boost us up to what's called a "high" or a "buzz." When the drugs wear off, however, we drop below our normal level of feeling. When we take drugs again, they boost us up, but never as high as the first time. When we come down, it's always lower than the last time. What eventually happens is that people end up taking drugs just to feel normal, the way you and I feel right now. Are drugs diamonds or zirconias? Definitely zirconias.

How about tobacco? We all know that you can't really be cool unless you're a "Marlboro Man," right? Wrong, and yet Satan would lead you to believe that smoking is cool and sophisticated.

Let me tell you about cool and sophisticated. A couple of years ago, I had a serious back problem and had to be hospitalized for a week. The first night I was in the hospital, I didn't get any sleep at all because I heard someone coughing and gagging the whole night. The next day, the nurse opened the door to my room and the door to the room across the hall from me. There in the bed lay a "Marlboro Man," and if he didn't look cool! He had designer tubes up his nose and was hooked up to a respirator. Why? Because he could not breathe on his own. He was dying of emphysema. What he had thought would bring joy and happiness he found out too late was a cheap imitation. Now he was reaping the rewards. Diamond or zirconia? Definitely a zirconia.

Alcohol probably has to be the most attractive zirconia of all. Don't you just love the ads and commercials? I have two favorites. The first is a liquor advertisement I found in a magazine: a picture of two great-looking guys at the top of a mountain getting ready to ski down. They are dressed in the latest styles, and their poles are planted and ready for the big take-off. The caption reads, "For those who really care." I don't know if you ski or not, but just imagine for a moment skiing down from the top of a mountain bombed out of your mind. I can see it now: you would be kissing every tree on the way down.

Then there are the beer commercials. Everybody is down at the local bar, where they are having a blast. Naturally, only the best-looking hunks are there, and, of course, only major foxes. They are singing their little songs. There they are, having the time of their lives. And what am I doing? Watching them have fun while I'm folding clothes or cleaning the kitchen. Even I am taken in sometimes. I think to myself, "Wow, is my life a drag or what? Hey, guys, count me in! I want to come on over and have a blast too!" Is alcohol a diamond or a zirconia, my young friend? Yes, it's a zirconia. Why? Because just once I wish the advertising companies would show you what happens after the party. Just once, I wish they would show you those cool dudes as they stumble out of the bar and throw up in the parking lot because they are sick from drinking so much beer. Just once I wish they would show you the railroad tracks across some cool dude's forehead where he had to be sewn up with stitches. Why? Because he was so drunk he couldn't see the top of the car as he got in and so he bashed in his forehead. And just once I would like them to show you the aftermath of a serious car accident in which someone you know was critically injured or killed—maybe someone in your school, maybe a friend of yours. Maybe someone in your family. Why? Because some cool dudes tied on one too many with the gang. Diamond or zirconia? Without a doubt, a zirconia.

Another zirconia that Satan throws out to you daily is immorality. The television and movies are loaded with it. Satan would have you believe that there's nothing wrong with sex as a natural way of showing someone that you really love them. He tells you, "It's a normal biological need, and if you are not expressing yourself sexually then there must be something seriously wrong with you!" Diamond or zirconia?

I remember being teased about being morally clean. When I was going to high school, I was the only girl in the school who was a Mormon, and everyone knew it. They knew what Mormons believe and that we do not participate in sex before marriage. But, you see, I had an additional problem. My name is Vivian; and Vivian, virtuous, and virgin all go together. I was known as Virtuous Vivian, the Big "V." I used to get teased all the time. I can still hear the football players as they would come up to me in the halls and ask, "Is it true? Are you really a virgin? You've got to be kidding! Are you frigid or something? You're not normal, you know." I used to get bugged about it all the time. I would usually just grin and bear it or say, "Oh, well." Finally, one day it just got to me. I had taken about all I could take. A cute basketball player came down the hall and said, "Hey, Big V, how ya doin'?"

That was it, the straw that broke the camel's back. Suddenly something in me just snapped! I grabbed the guy's shirt with my fist at his neck and thumped him against the lockers. I looked him straight in the face and said, "Yes, I'm virtuous and clean. But let me tell you something, buddy: It's not any easier for me than it is for you because I have the same passions and desires that you have. But one of these days, I'm going to find someone and get married—not for a couple of years to see if it works but for an eternity. Then I am going to take every one of those passions and *unleash them all!*" Not only did that guy quit teasing me, but from that time on he began to defend me. If anyone would say, "Hey, Big V," he would say, "Shut up, man, she's cool." Diamond or zirconia? Actually, within the bounds of marriage, sex is a priceless diamond. But outside the bounds of marriage, immorality in any of its forms is a zirconia that can bring much sadness.

Every day of your life, you will have to decide between diamonds and zirconias. How can you tell the difference? At the jewelry counter, I couldn't see the difference. I asked a friend of mine who owned a jewelry company how he could tell the difference, and he said, "You can't. The only way a jeweler can tell is with a special magnifying glass called a loupe."

So how can we decide between life's diamonds or zirconias? We, too, have special help. Our loupe is called the Holy Ghost. He will help us see the difference between what is real and eternal and what is false and momentary. All you have to do is ask for his help.

A couple of years ago, my husband and I went to see a movie. In the film, the villain was introduced in one of the most unusual ways I have ever seen. The character was dressed just like everybody else, and he was standing in the center of a group of people outside of a house. As the movie camera passed across the crowd, we saw the villain, but we did not know he was the villain. The camera did not pause or move closer. However, the minute I saw this character, chills ran down my spine. I looked at Doug, my husband. He looked at me. I said, "Wow, did they pick the right guy for that part." Doug said, "That has to be the villain. That guy is really evil." The movie camera again slowly panned the same people, but this time when it got to the man we had seen, sure enough, he was introduced as the villain of the film.

So we had outguessed the director of the movie. "No big deal," I thought until a week later when I was looking through a national magazine and saw a picture of the same man. He was the lead singer of a famous hard-rock group. As I read the article about this man and the evil he espouses, my original feelings about him were confirmed. Did I prejudge this man? No. I had no idea who he was. All I knew was that something was amiss in his life. How did I know? My jeweler's loupe. The Holy Ghost will help you feel what is good or bad if you will but stay close to the Lord.

When I was younger, I attended several different colleges. At one particular college was a young man for whom the words *good looking* were invented. He was probably the best-looking man I had ever seen (until I met my husband!). He was about 6'4" tall with light blue eyes, a flawless complexion, pearly white teeth, beautiful dimples, wide shoulders, and narrow hips. He was the kind of man that made girls stop, stare, and say, "It lives, it breathes, it walks." Even when the other guys on campus saw him, they would say, "It's disgusting." Not only was he good looking, but he was also filthy rich. His father was the vice-president of a multi-billion dollar conglomerate in the East, and Stan was indeed born with a silver spoon in his mouth. He had the best of everything—the best governesses, the best nannies, and the best tutors. He was also talented. He was the starting pitcher for the school baseball team. Some would say Stan had it all.

One day a friend of mine who knew Stan said, "Hey, Vivian, would you like to meet Stan?"

"Does the sun rise?" I said.

Shortly thereafter the opportunity arose, and I got to meet *the* man on campus. I can still remember not being able to sleep for three days.

We ended up at a party together—little ol' me and the entire tennis team, football team, and, of course, baseball team. It was better than being in Baskin-Robbins. I had never seen so many different flavors in my life. There was French vanilla, chocolate, strawberry, and Neapolitan. My eyes could not believe what they saw. I looked at all their gorgeous faces, then their gorgeous shoulders, and then their hands, and suddenly shock went through my entire body. Everyone, including Stan, was holding a can of beer. I took one look at those beer cans, and suddenly something inside me said, "Vivian, get out of here. You don't belong here." Then I had second thoughts. "Now wait a minute. Don't be such a prude. Just because you have standards doesn't mean that you have to inflict them upon the rest of the world. You can set a good example for them. And besides, see how good looking they are!" I let my poor judgment overrule and decided to stay for just a few minutes.

Stan started walking with me, and we talked. As we walked, in one room I saw a marijuana party in full percolation. I had seen enough. I looked at Stan and said, "Would you please take me home?" Stan looked puzzled. "Why?"

"I would like to go now, please."

"All right."

Very reluctantly, Stan gathered his things and took me home. I thought I'd really made a bad first impression until I heard from Stan again. I picked up the phone.

"Hello."

Stan said, "Hello, Vivian. It's Stan. How are you?" My heart must have started pounding a million beats a minute.

"Fine," I managed to squeak.

He said, "Vivian, I have tickets to the Governor's Ball, and I want to take you."

Do you know how hard it is to get such tickets? It's one of the most posh social events of the year. The tickets are extremely expensive, and here Stan had asked me to this big event. He said, "I'll have my limousine pick you up at 7:00." Suddenly, visions of grandeur flashed through my mind. The Governor's Ball, a limousine, I'll wear a formal. All I need is a pair of glass slippers and I'll be just like Cinderella. Then the reality of the situation hit me. I knew his standards and I knew mine. I very quietly said, "I can't go, Stan. I already have plans for that night." (I do wash my hair occasionally.)

He, being the jock he was, quickly responded with, "So . . . break them."

I can still feel the pressure I felt that night as I said, "I can't, Stan."

"Are you sure?" I knew exactly what he meant.

"Yes," I said, and he knew exactly what I meant. I never heard from Stan again.

About five years ago, I was at a social event where I saw the guy that had introduced me to Stan. Of course, I quickly ran up to him, said hello, and asked him about his wife and family. He told me that his wife was there, so I went over to visit with her for a few minutes. In the course of our conversation, I asked her if they had kept up with Stan. She said yes they had, so I pursued the conversation. When I asked her how he was and if he had married and had a million kids, she became very sober. "Vivian," she said, "Stan is a kept man." Somehow that didn't surprise me. Stan always had a weakness for the easy life. I chuckled and said, "Yeah, I can just see Stan living with some rich woman." My friend didn't laugh. She looked at me with graveness in her face as she said, "Vivian, it's not a woman." My heart sank right down to my feet. I couldn't believe what I had heard. "You're lying to me," I said. "I don't believe that for a minute."

She said, "It's true, Vivian."

How in the world could something like this happen to someone who had it all? Still in shock, I asked my friend if she ever saw him.

"Stan came over recently to visit us. His family has completely disowned him, so we are about the only old friends he has." My friend went on, "Last time we saw him, Stan came out to our home. He's never done that before. You know he looks different now. Remember that gorgeous skin he had? Now it's beginning to look wrinkly and weathered. And remember his beautiful blond hair? It's starting to recede on his forehead. Well, we don't have a lot of money, Vivian. We live in a modest split-entry home. As Stan walked in wearing his expensive silk suit and his heavy gold chains and jewelry, he looked around at our humble circumstances and said, 'Do you know what? I really envy you guys.' " Big tears came into Stan's eyes as he slowly left their home.

What happened to my friend Stan? I'll tell you what happened. Every time he had to choose between diamonds and zirconias, he made the wrong choice. He would never look deep enough to distinguish between the two.

It doesn't have to be like that, my friend. Stay in tune with the Spirit. You will be able to see the difference clearly. In Jacob 4:13, we are promised, "The Spirit speaketh the truth and lieth not. . . . It speaketh of things as they really are, and of things as they really will be." By using our jeweler's loupe, we will not be deceived by counterfeits but will see things as they really are. As you stay worthy of his influence, the Holy Ghost will guide you. This is a promise.

I leave you my testimony that the gospel is true, that The Church of Jesus Christ of Latter-day Saints is the true church that our Father in heaven has so graciously restored to the earth in these latter days to give us guidance and direction to be able to return to his presence. I love it with every beat of my heart and every fiber of my being.

Vivian Cline is director of the BYU Youth and Family Program's "Polish with Pleasure" workshop. She has modeled professionally for fifteen years and teaches modeling, poise, and etiquette. She is a former Mrs. Utah America. She and her husband, S. Douglas Cline, have five children.

Chapter 6

Teen Trials and Triumphs

Suzanne Hansen

Life for teenagers does have its ups and downs. In fact, it's much like a roller coaster, full of thrilling highs—and depressing lows. In the pre-earth life, God explained it all, and we voted to come. Despite the hardships and difficulties, we knew that this life would be worth the test! Eternal life—what a prize!

Now that you're here, you're starting to wonder, "Is it worth it?" Yes, it is. But I hear you say, "Well, if only I had a better looking body, or if only I was smarter, or if only I had a date for Friday night, or if only I had some new clothes, I'd feel better about me. And I'd be a whole lot happier too."

All these things may bring you just a minute of happiness but not forever happiness. The things that will bring you forever happiness are those of the heart and spirit, like the knowledge that you are a child of God—and God doesn't make mistakes—especially on you! He had a purpose sending you here and a reason for making you just the way you are. He gave you what you needed to be successful and happy. "I know that," you say, "but it's a lot tougher than I thought!" I know how you feel, but I know God plans for you to succeed.

When I was a child, I asked my grandpa, who was much smarter than I, where I got my belly button. "I have it on the best authority," he joked. "I remember that in heaven, after God created us all, he put us on a conveyor belt, and we rode down into the inspection chamber. There we were checked over from head to toe to see if were were done. When he saw that you were done, he pushed your belly, and that's your 'done' button. You're all done—you've got everything you need to be a success in life and to be happy."

We all have what we need to be successful on earth, even if times are sometimes difficult. Our problem is, we spend 89 percent of our time thinking about how unsuccessful, unhappy, and ugly we are.

I've never met a person who hasn't thought he or she wasn't ugly or stupid at one time or another. The problem is, if those thoughts stay long enough, they will destroy the greatest in you, *so get rid of them fast!* Just realize that negative thoughts are Satan's way of getting you down, putting you down, and bringing you down to hell. He wants you to feel as bad as he does, so don't give in. Start thinking positively. I've found that life is just as happy and successful as I make it.

Take control and make happiness happen. Think good, happy, uplifting thoughts. Start by thinking about the successful things you do daily. Then realize you have no one to blame but yourself if today doesn't turn out. You're in the driver's seat, and you determine your destiny—not your parents, not your peers, not your teachers—not the magazines, movies, or billboards. You're a great and wonderful person, one with talents and skills just waiting to be used.

I have children of my own, and I know how hard growing up is. After all, I grew up, and I've watched the hard times my kids have had. I feel sure that God told us before we left heaven: "Remember, I love you. Life on earth won't be easy, but it will be worth it all. Good luck. Keep in touch!"

As my earthly family struggled one morning, it made me realize how much we blame others for the choices we ourselves are free to make. After breakfast, I tried as hard as I could to hurry my kids along. My son John was slow and uncooperative. I kept saying, "Hurry, you'll be late," but he moved like a turtle. We rushed to the car without a moment

65

to spare. John turned and yelled as we drove to school, "Mom, if you had been in the car waiting, I wouldn't have been late for school." I looked at him in amazement and said, "John, when I'm dead, who are you going to blame?" John made his choice to be slow and not to help, but he wouldn't take the responsibility for that choice.

We need to stop looking for someone to blame for our unhappiness or loneliness or depression. If *you* are unhappy or sad or feel unliked or uncared about, it may be because of your choices.

You can lift your life and be happy. You can be happier today by doing a few small things, like praying. Pray for ability to see past the storms of everyday living and to gain an eternal perspective. Ask yourself before you get upset, "How will this affect my eternity?" Before you know it, things that once made you so uptight and upset won't seem so important.

One young lady told of an experience that helped her see a purpose for her life. Karen states, "In March of 1974 I was very busy, hurrying to make preparations to go to Nauvoo with my seminary class. It was spring vacation. How exciting it was! This was the trip everyone had looked forward to and planned for.

"On Monday, April 1, four young classmates were riding with me in a Volkswagen van driven by our teacher and bishop, Don Richards. The four young men in our group were following us in a green Oldsmobile. We reached Carthage, the town where the Prophet Joseph Smith and his brother Hyrum met their deaths. We toured the jail room in which they were killed. I couldn't believe how strong the Spirit was in that room. It really impressed me.

"By the time we reached Nauvoo, all of the old edifices were closed. We drove through nearby parks and found a place to camp for the night. The park was beautiful, with a green forest all around. The young men pitched tents to sleep in, and all the girls got to sleep in a fold-down camper. We spent the evening enjoying one another's company and having a great time. The next day was beautiful, and the sun was bright as it came up. We all walked together about old Nauvoo and looked in the old windows. The town had so much history. I could just imagine what it might have been like. I really enjoyed the day and what we saw. That night, again we pitched camp. What fun it was to get to know each other and share such a spiritual day.

"The next morning we quickly ate and rushed to get everything cleaned up and put away. We then visited the beautiful Nauvoo Temple foundations, although the temple no longer stood. A special peaceful feeling was there. Our teacher, who was wise and spiritual, stood on a slightly raised piece of ground and said, 'I get chills just looking at this sacred piece of land where the Lord once stood.' How wonderful it seemed to walk where the Prophet Joseph had once walked. My testimony was renewed although I was only seventeen. I promised the Lord I would help spread the gospel to his children.

"The following day, we broke camp after a wonderful night's sleep—well, what sleep we got was great. We ate and had prayer. We were on our way by 9:00 A.M. As we traveled, we were singing, giggling, and talking like most girls do. This trip helped us grow closer to each other.

"About 4:30 P.M. we all took a nap. About 5:15 I was awakened, and Bishop Richards said that we were just leaving Monticello, Indiana, eighty miles west of our homes. It seemed unusually dark and dreary. Then someone remarked that we had just missed a very bad storm. We were driving over a bridge when suddenly it seemed like huge buckets of water were coming down on us from nowhere. Something was hitting the van. One of the girls yelled, 'It's hailing!' 'No, no,' our teacher said. 'Those are sticks and stones blowing into our car!'

"How well I remember the fear that rose up inside me, and my friends looked so frightened. My thought was, 'Oh, no, I'm going to die,' yet I knew deep down I wasn't going to. Our teacher said with a commanding voice, 'Get down on the floor.' We all did what he said. Then I felt the van being picked up—we were going around and around.

"Everyone was now screaming in terror. 'Is someone in pain?' I thought. The car was moving as the storm shook it. I thought my friend was hurt. In the midst of all the fear and frustration, the Spirit whispered, 'Put your arms up over your head.' I did so quickly.

"My seat was by the back window, and the window was suddenly gone. When I first felt the water, I thought that we had been flooded. Suddenly water was everywhere. Where did it come from? This all seemed like a terrible nightmare, and I was just waiting for it to end. I found myself swimming. I swam right out of the van. Then I realized that we had gone off the bridge into a river. Later, I heard that the van had been picked up by a tornado. We had dropped fifty feet into the Tippecanoe River, nose first. We suddenly heard a loud crash, and the van was completely submerged. Great gusts of wind and large waves hit us and hurled us five or more feet through the air. We were all helpless before the forces of nature. The storm and the undercurrents were ferocious. I felt helpless. I could see that my friends were weak. They must have had head injuries—they seemed unable to help themselves. The current whipped me ten feet away from them, and the waves seemed to force them farther and farther from my sight. My heart ached for them. I wanted to help them, but I could hardly help myself. I began choking because of the lashing, whipping currents of water. They crashed against my body and face with such force that I couldn't get a breath. My lungs started to ache for want of air. All at once, my eyes caught sight of a concrete bridge support. I knew if I could somehow make it that far, I would have a small chance. If only I could hold on until the storm passed! The current seemed to become ever stronger. The strength in my limbs was weakening. I felt helpless and at the mercy of this storm. I started to feel there was no use in trying. The waves were so powerful they seemed to be pulling me in two different directions. Thoughts of Joseph Smith passed through my mind. Then a picture of Christ and the crucifixion. It gave me strength to face my death.

"I prayed as I had never prayed before in my life, 'Please, Lord, keep me from drowning, please, please.' I pleaded, 'I'm not ready to die, Lord.' As a large wave struck my body, the Spirit again spoke peace to my soul. I seemed to hear the words, 'Swim on your back. Keep your head and face up.' And then came this prompting:, 'Swallow the water when it comes. Don't panic. Don't panic.' I swallowed the water as it hit my face as the violent storm raged on. I could at last breathe.

"Subsequently, I swallowed and regurgitated what seemed like gallons of water. The rough currents accompanied by monstrous waves continued. At this point, weak and sick, I decided that I could not take any more. I could not win this fight. My prayer changed. I began asking, 'Heavenly Father, please take me home to you and peace and love.' I wanted to be released from the pains and trials of life, and the pains in my head became so intense that all my body cried for release. 'I want to die, dear God.' My body started to give in to the storm. I found myself floating face first in the water. Then all of a sudden something clicked in my shattered mind. And I found myself talking to myself.

" 'You dummy, as long as you have a fighting chance and life, keep fighting.' I once more tried to arouse all my faculties, and with every bit of strength, I turned on my back and gasped for air. I had won the battle against myself, and now I must win against the elements. At that moment, the elements no longer raged. The winds, the waves, and the rains stopped as if the Lord had touched them and commanded them to stop! I heard a voice once again. This time it was loud and clear: 'Karen, you shall not die. Your mission on earth is not yet completed.'

"The Spirit stayed with me and strengthened my weakened body and enabled me to swim to a concrete pier. The swim took about ten minutes or more. I swam the distance on my back. A small tree limb bumped against my head. Everything was so foggy in my mind. I grabbed it to keep afloat, then used it to pull myself out of the cold, frothy water. As I sat on the side of the river, my thoughts suddenly raced, and I looked into the water to see my friends. I saw no one, and I realized that all five of my friends were probably underwater. They must have drowned! Oh, no, how could this be? A flood of emotion welled up inside me. I found myself wild with emotion, screaming, filled with great sorrow. I was in hysterics. Tears felt like rain running from my eyes. 'My friends, my friends, where are they?' I cried. I decided that I needed to get help. I somehow found a woman. She was very kind. She cared for me until the state highway patrol trooper came. The men in the area had organized themselves and began to search for my friends. Night fell quickly, and all searching was halted.

"I was taken to a nearby hospital. As I waited, my mind's eye took me back to the faces of my friends just before the storm hit. Would this nightmare end? I was quickly released and taken to Logansport to the home of an LDS branch president. I was so grateful to receive a blessing. The Spirit comforted me. When I went to bed, sleep came as peacefully as the branch president had said it would. I was so grateful for the priesthood of God and its power to comfort.

"I remember as the morning came, I thought, 'It's a miracle—I'm alive!' As I waited for word on my friends, I was suffering from shock. I repeatedly fought back the tears and emotions as I asked about my friends. I was assured by a veteran trooper that the police were doing everything possible. I felt helpless. I kept praying for my friends.

"Not until two weeks after the tornado hit did they find my friends. Sharon Mill's body was floating in Lake Freeman. The civil defense workers dragged the Tippecanoe River to find five other victims. I was the only one to survive. I couldn't believe it—only the day before, we were laughing, singing, and loving life, just teenagers with no fear of death or tragedy.

"Later I heard that the winds had been in excess of five hundred miles an hour, and I had been in the middle of this storm of fury. Today, I'm very grateful for a loving Heavenly Father who saw fit to leave me here on earth. I also know that my friends were needed on the other side for God's work, for they are all wonderful people, and I love them and miss them."

Just as Karen had to battle a giant of a storm, we also have storms of life that try and test our faith and endurance and limits. These storms may not be seen by the human eye, but they rage within each of us. This is the battle of our spirits against the forces of evil. Those storms at times move in slowly, and often they strike without warning. They can blind our spiritual eyes from seeing the realities of eternal life and the value God sees in each of his children. We find ourselves being tossed and turned by the world and all its influences. Before you is a storm. You're in the middle of the greatest of all storms, the storm of negativeness, and then you find yourself being hit by the great waves of despair, sadness, discontent, depression, and discouragement. You drown in your self-pity. These waves of temptation are self-indulgence, unhappiness, selfishness, and self-pity, and they are just as life threatening and just as real and powerful as the forceful winds of a devastating tornado.

But, no matter what stormy crisis comes your way, you can swim to safety by following the teachings and example set by our Savior. Use the examples Jesus Christ gave. He taught us, by his example, that we can weather any storm that may come our way.

The guidelines he gave will help us reach dry land and eternal joy. He taught us, "Love thy neighbor as thyself," not to be blinded by our needs and wants and ignore the needs of others, by finding faults and cutting down others. This wave of temptation will make us unhappy and lonely.

In loving yourself and seeing the good in you, you can see the good in others and love them truly. And at the same time, you learn to love yourself in an unselfish way. The Lord taught about unselfishness when he taught, "Feed my sheep." He didn't say, "Starve others from your love if you don't see eye-to-eye with them or agree with them or know them." He simply said, "Feed my sheep." That means you should feed others with your strength and love. We are all sheep of his fold. You can start by smiling at people. You can lift the spirits of another person. If you give a word of encouragement, you do as Christ asked. When you feed his sheep, your actions, no matter how small, make a difference.

I know this life seems overwhelming, but I also know that if you live what you know to be true, the windows of heaven will be opened, and the Lord will bless you richly in school, in friendships, in whatever you seek in righteousness. No effort goes unrecognized by the Lord.

A young man of only eighteen years of age, Russell Richardson, held true to the teachings of Christ even through the storms and trials of life. He was serving as student-body president of his school when he was diagnosed as having cancer. But he always kept a good attitude. A friend said of him, "I will always remember his positive attitude and example. It will help me the rest of my life!"

Russ was not able to serve in his office the way he wanted to because of five operations to remove cancer. Then three chemotherapy treatments left him weak and sometimes unable to go to school. But he was a hard worker and would do his best no matter what. He served that year and lifted the lives of others as he weathered his storms of illness and pain. When Russ gave the final speech at high-school graduation, he told his classmates about three keys to ensure success: family, religion, and friends. When he completed his speech, the whole senior class gave him a standing ovation. This speech was a miracle, as a few months before, Russell had suffered a severe flair-up of cancer in his spine and was

72

told he'd never live until graduation. But he willed himself to live and wouldn't give in.

At his death, just months later, fifteen hundred students gathered to pay tribute to their friend. Rarely has such a young person earned and received the respect given Russell. In view of his death, the high school immediately made plans to change their schedule and make his funeral a priority. Sporting events were canceled. The flag was flown at half mast, and the "V" on the mountain was lit as a symbol of the light Russell had brought into the students' lives. Yes, for one so young to be so revered is a tribute to his great courage and character.

Russell had written a message that he wanted read at the funeral. As his friend Mark began reading the message, a hush fell over the congregation. Mark's voice cracked with emotion as he began: "I imagine that this is the very first funeral ever to have the deceased person take part on the program. This may seem strange, but, as you know, I always like to do things in a strange way.

"I feel this an appropriate time to express my love and appreciation and gratitude to my family and friends. I could not ask for a more supportive, caring, and understanding family. I love you all very much.

"To my friends, I want each one of you to know that you have greatly contributed to the quality of my life. I have really valued your friendship. You have been there through all the ups and downs and have endured all the garbage that I dished out. You came through for me, and I can't tell you how much I appreciate it.

"I would like to thank you for coming. I appreciate all of the fasting and prayers on my behalf. I want you to know I am finally at peace with myself and very, very happy. I look forward to the day when I can see each of you again."

Mark then added, "If Russell had no other mission in this life than to make us grateful for our lives, he passed the test with flying colors. It was a great privilege and honor to know him. I will not forget him or what he stood for, and I'd love to tell his parents he was just as good a person away from home as he was with his family."

Then the principal shared with the audience this quotation: "There is no tragedy in suffering, only tragedy in suffering in vain." Russell, a young man of seventeen, did not suffer in vain. He was victorious over the trials of his life. His philosophy of life is perhaps best described in the last line of his farewell message to his family and friends that day. "I want each of you to give me a big smile right now!"

Just as these two young people endured the storms of life that tested them to the limit and beyond, by staying in tune with the spirit of God, we too can endure. Then and only then can we find true happiness and joy.

Our lives can be saved by clinging to the teachings of God and his Son, who are the life preservers for *all* people. Then and only then can we feel better about ourselves and find true and *lasting* happiness and success. So when the stormy challenges of this world get you down, turn your face toward the heavens and ask for help. Heavenly Father will help you too because you are a child of God, and he loves you and has faith that you too can succeed.

Suzanne Hansen is the founder and president of Su-Z Enterprises. She has worked as a newspaper columnist and has appeared on many TV talk shows. She was Utah's Honor Mother in 1980 and was recognized as one of the Outstanding Young Women in America in 1984 and 1985. She and her husband, Michael, have three children.

Chapter 7

How to Ruin a Romance

Barbara Barrington Jones

When I talk to high-school classes, I always ask both boys and girls for their pet peeves about the opposite sex. I ask what bothers girls about guys and what bothers guys about girls. The answers always come in the same ways. The girls are quick to answer first. The guys never say anything until the end, but they have an equally long list. I thought it might be revealing to see the things that cause problems in dating.

Girls' Pet Peeve #1. The guy calls up a girl for a date, and the conversation goes something like this:

"Hi, Judy, this is Tim. How about a date?"

Judy answers, "That sounds like fun."

Then Tim asks, "What do you want to do?"

They begin to go back and forth. "No, what do *you* want to do?"

"I don't know. What do you want to do?"

"No really, you decide. Let's do what you want to do."

The thing goes on and on.

Guys, the girl is trying to get you to decide. You need to present a plan.

Guys' Pet Peeve #1. A boy and a girl are driving along or sitting somewhere together. The guy thinks that they are enjoying a comfortable silence when the girl asks, "What's wrong?"

He answers truthfully, "Nothing."

The girl presses, "No, really, what's wrong?"

"Nothing's wrong."

"No, really, I know there's something wrong."

The guy finally thinks, "There's nothing wrong, but there's going to be pretty soon."

Girls, resist over-analyzing everything. Guys do not feel the need to examine a dating relationship with as much thoroughness as girls do.

Girls' Pet Peeve #2. A girl hates it when the guy shows up late for a date. Guys, I'm going to tell you a terrific strategy for making points with a girl's parents.

First, show up on time. When you walk in, shake hands with both the mother and father and, as a way of introduction, say, "How do you do. My name is ————." They will be pleasantly impressed by your good manners.

Second, when the girl comes in, say "Susan, you look really nice tonight." She'll fall dead in her tracks when you say that.

Then this is the clincher—this will make the parents love you. Ask her parents, "What time would you like for me to have your daughter in tonight?"

I'm not kidding you. The minute you leave the room, the dad is going to say, "Now that's the kind of young man my daughter should be out with."

Guys' Pet Peeve #2. When the guy shows up on time, do not make him wait. He has already said what he needs to with your parents. The conversation becomes uncomfortable. Don't make him wait.

Girls' Pet Peeve #3. A girl hates it when a boy says, "I'll call you" and then doesn't.

Often a guy doesn't even realize that he is saying it. But a girl takes it seriously. She will sit by the phone and wait. It is very upsetting. If you say you're going to call, then call. If you're not going to call, don't say it.

I have asked guys if it is okay for girls to call them. The answer was both yes and no. The guys that date a lot say no: "We want to be the ones that initiate the call. But after we have been going with a girl, it's great. It's fine to call."

The shy guys, however, say "We love it. We think it's great for a girl to call us."

Guys hate:

A girl who talks all the time about nothing.

Too much perfume.

Too much makeup. If you are wondering if you have too much makeup on, you do.

Getting makeup on their clothes.

A girl who won't talk.

Girls hate:

Music in the car so loud that you can't talk.

Too much aftershave.

Shaving stubble.

The mirror syndrome. (Every time a guy walks past a mirror, he has to check himself out.)

A time-warp hairstyle.

A guy who only wears sweats.

A guy who dresses exactly like all his friends.

A guy's main problem is his ego. If you bruise that, it's all over. A girl's main problem is that she loves to analyze everything. She will analyze and reanalyze with her girl-friends and her mom.

Dating is a great way to get to know and enjoy being around a lot of different people. However, here are a few surefire ways to kill a budding romance:

1. Be a policeman or policewoman. Get upset if the person you are interested in is seen talking to anyone else. Act as if the person is your private property and you don't want any-one else being around the person.

2. Playing hard to get and other games. If one person does all the giving and the other doesn't respond in kind, the romance is not going to work.

3. Talk about commitment on the first date. Try to analyze where things are going on the first date. Chances are a guy doesn't even know yet.

4. Love a guy only when he is feeling strong. Everyone should be allowed to have a bad day occasionally.

5. Take him or her for granted.

6. Open old wounds. Rub it in about an old girlfriend or boyfriend. Bring up the past, who the person dated and what the person did.

7. Get hung up on three little words. For some people it is very easy to say "I love you." For others it is really hard.

8. Be everywhere together, between classes, at lunch, after school. Smother the person with your presence every moment.

I was talking at a high school one day when I noticed some tension going on between a girl and her boyfriend. She read a note that he handed her, wadded it up, and threw it in the trash. After they left, I retrieved the note. This is what it said:

"I understand you. This is a definite sign that you are getting tired of me. You can't tell me it isn't. There are many examples:

"1. You don't like me anymore.

"2. You don't like to talk to me on the phone or even call me.

"3. (scribbled out)

"4. You don't like to be with me all the time. It's obvious you are getting tired of me, and I'm sorry you are. You say you love me and I believe you, but I know that you are sick of me. I predict that within a month you'll break up with me, but I think you'll regret it eventually. You expect me not to be mad that you don't like me all the time, but how would you feel if you called me tonight to go to the glee club thing and I said well, no, I didn't want to go. I just don't feel like seeing you. This is no big deal, I know. I knew it would eventually happen like this. It happens to all relationships when they get to the end.

"I love you. I wish you loved me as much. Our relationship would be perfect. I know that I didn't buy you presents and flowers all the time, but I tried.

"P.S. I don't want anyone else to read this.

"P.P.S. Why don't you write me back. What do you mean you don't have paper? You could have taken a ten-minute time-out. I guess I can't change you.

"Well, I don't mean this letter. I'm just in a bad mood. I'm fighting with you. I'm getting F's on everything. I don't do my homework. My dad's after me. I'm doing terrible in track. Why is everything going so bad for me?"

Could you have written this letter? Take this quiz and see how your self-image stacks up.

1. Is how you feel about yourself based on what others say about you?

A girl or guy comes up to you and says, "Gee, you look great today." Do you think, "How can they say I look great today? They're just saying that. I really don't."

If you think like that, you're a one.

If you would say, "Thanks," and mean it, you're a ten.

2. You go out and buy a brand new outfit. You think you look terrific. When you wear it, the first thing your friend says is, "Where did you get that?"

If you say to yourself, "I'm never going to wear this again," you're a one.

If you say to yourself, "I like it. I spent a lot of time picking this out," you're a ten.

3. How you feel about yourself is based on how well you do things.

Your parents want you to make A's and B's on your report card. If you do, they promise you a reward.

You do your very best, and you get one C. How do you feel about yourself? If you are totally bummed out, you're a one.

If you say to yourself, "Look, I did my very best; there was no way I could have done any better," you are a ten.

And if you can go to your parents and honestly say that, you are a ten plus.

4. Can you show your feelings to people?

Your parents accuse you of something you did not do. If you can stick up for yourself without going into a temper tantrum, then you're a ten. Or if you turn around and walk into your room and slam the door, saying, "They should know that I didn't," then you're a one.

5. Can you let people know what your weaknesses are?

If you can let your boyfriend see you without any makeup on, you're a ten. If you look awful, and when your boyfriend comes to the door you don't answer it, then you're a one.

If you're a guy, can you let a girl see you cry? If you can't you're a one. If you can, you're a ten.

6. How you feel about yourself depends on the way you look. If you look in the mirror and say, "Not bad; I like you," then you're a ten.

If you look in the mirror and say, "Why me?" you're a one.

7. Do you compare your situation with others? You're a ten if you can say, "You know, I wouldn't trade with any-body." You're a one if you say, "I wish I were Ted or Susan. I wish I could play the piano like Jane. I wish I looked like Beth."

How do we develop more self-esteem? How do we feel better about ourselves? Remember this, God did not forget you. You have special talents, special abilities that nobody else has. It's up to you to find out what they are. *What you are is a gift from God. What you become is your gift to him.*

As you grow in confidence, then you can stop looking inward at yourself and look out at the rest of the world. When you truly become unselfish, then you can become more com-fortable in dating and getting to know new friends. Forgetting yourself and thinking about the other person first is perhaps the greatest secret not only to successful dating but also to a successful life.

Barbara Barrington Jones grooms young women for the Miss Universe, Miss USA, Miss America, and Junior Miss beauty pageants. She spent twenty-five years in classical ballet and has been a fashion designer and professional model. She and her husband, Hal, have two children. They live in Novato, California.

Chapter 8

Trekking that Trying, Trembling, Tremendous Trail toward Testimony or How to Come to Know "I Know!"

Jack S. Marshall

If a person has a problem with the Word of Wisdom, chastity, paying tithing, keeping the Sabbath, inactivity— whatever the problem is, that's not the problem; it's a symptom of the problem. Similarly, if you have a runny nose, coughing, sneezing, and drippy eyes, those things are not the problem; they are symptoms of the problem. The problem is that you have a cold. The runny nose and other things are manifestations of that cold. So if a person has problems keeping the commandments, the real problem is the level of the person's faith and testimony.

I'd like to share with you some ways to distinguish where you are in your testimony and how to increase your faith. As you do, you'll find better actions in your life and have greater joy and hope as you work through this schooling period called mortality.

The study of faith and testimony can be complex. I want to make it simple. Modern Christianity has taken too many wonderfully simple concepts and made them unrecognizable. I read in a newspaper not too long ago a small article that says so very well what modern Christendom has done to many wonderful, simple concepts. It spoke of graffiti on a wall at a religious university that read: "Jesus said unto them, Who

do you say that I am? And they replied: You are the escha-
tological manifestation of the ground of our being, the ker-
ygma in which we find the ultimate meaning of our inter-
personal relationship. And Jesus said: What?"

Let's study about faith and testimony and make it simple
so there's no misunderstanding. Faith as defined in the Book
of Mormon "is not to have a perfect knowledge of things;
therefore if ye have faith ye hope for things which are not
seen, which are true." (Alma 32:21.)

Here's the hypothesis, then: We are taught some things
that are true or real but that are unseen to us, and faith is to
develop a hope or belief in those unseen realities. Simple
enough?

What are some of those unseen realities you're taught to
believe in? In fact, you're banking your whole life on the fact
that they are true, though you do not see them. How about
God the Father and Jesus Christ? If you've seen them lately,
you can stop reading this chapter on how to develop faith.
Other unseen realities to you may be the resurrection, the
three degrees of glory, and the fact that families are forever.

There are three elements that will enable you to develop
faith and testimony. First, you must have hope that what
you're taught is true. Second, you must act on the truth. Jesus
said: "If any man will do his will, he shall know of the doctrine,
whether it be of God, or whether I speak of myself." (John
7:17.) James said "Faith, if it hath not works, is dead." (James
2:17.) There must be action. By acting upon the teaching, we
come to know if it is true or not.

The third element is best described in D&C 82:10: "I, the
Lord, am bound when ye do what I say; but when ye do not
what I say, ye have no promise." The promise is that if we
do what we should, Father is bound to give us evidences
of unseen things, assurances of those unseen realities. In
short, we'll receive confirmations that will increase our hope
of unseen things, which will in turn increase our proper
actions.

83

There you have it, the way to develop testimony and faith. The three key ingredients are hope, proper actions, and receiving confirmations.

There are four levels as we grow in knowledge of those unseen things. The first level begins with the hope that the gospel is true—we don't know it's true—we just hope it is.

When I was nineteen years old and lived in Japan, two wonderful young men in dark suits knocked on my door and introduced themselves. They both had the same first name, Elder and Elder. I invited them in. That night, they taught me where I came from, why I was here, and what I could accomplish by living certain principles.

They taught me about a young man named Joseph Smith who had prayed fervently and come to know that God the Father and Jesus Christ existed and about the restoration of the gospel. As they left that evening, I realized I had never before heard such wonderful things.

Did I know what they said was true? No! I thought to myself, "That's marvelous! I hope it's true!" That's the beginning of faith and testimony.

Now the action level. Alma talks about certain actions that will help faith grow. He says, "Awake and arouse your faculties, even to an experiment upon my words . . . even if you can no more than desire, let this desire work in you." (Alma 32:27.) Exercise a particle of faith, for only after the action will you receive confirmation of these unseen realities.

Not too long ago, I was teaching at a Know Your Religion conference in Northern California. I had finished up on Saturday night, and on Sunday I went to church before returning home. It was a marvelous fast and testimony meeting.

As I was sitting in this meeting, Saints stood up and bore their witness, and then we had a wonderful experience. There was a black man in the audience. He got up and walked to the pulpit, his eyes brimming with tears. He started to speak and immediately caught our attention because he spoke with a thick accent in broken English. He was from Ethiopia. The

first thing he said was, "I am not a member of your church."
(I was seated next to the full-time elders in the congregation.
Their eyes kind of bulged out of their heads.) He continued:
"I will tell you why I am here today. Two nights ago, late at
night, I am driving home. I see a man and a woman. They
are standing by their car doing like this." (He motioned with
his thumb as if he were hitchhiking.) "I did not pick them up
because I was afraid if I picked them up they would beat upon
my face." (He was afraid of getting mugged. He had been
taught that you don't pick up strangers. But this was a very
isolated road, and we later learned that the couple's car had
broken down and the only way they could get home was for
this man to pick them up.) "I did not pick them up. But a
voice, it speaks to my mind. It says go and pick them up. So
I go and pick them up."

He turned the car around, went back, and offered them
a ride. As he offered them a ride, the woman stepped behind
her husband for protection from the stranger in the car. He
could read the non-verbal communication. Quickly he responded, "Do not be afraid. I am a Christian." Only after he
had announced he was a Christian did the couple feel comfortable enough to get into the car with him. Now this incident
wasn't coincidence—the couple just happened to be Latter-
day Saints. What a great opportunity to do some missionary
work!

As they drove into town, the husband said, "You say
you're a Christian; what church do you belong to?"

"I don't belong to any church; I love studying the life of
Jesus Christ from the holy scriptures."

He replied, "While you're here in America, would you
like to attend our church?"

"I would be honored."

Then, as only Latter-day Saints can, the couple took out
a sheet of paper and quickly wrote down the address of the
LDS meetinghouse and the times sacrament meeting began.
They said, "Go at this time; if you don't like this time, go at

85

this time; and if you don't like that time, go at this time; and if you don't like that time . . . "

We love meetings in this church. If we had a 14th Article of Faith, it would most likely read: "We believe in meetings, we hope for meetings, we have endured many meetings and hope to be able to endure all meetings. If there is any reason, excuse, or justification for having a meeting, we seek after it."

Now a few days later, this marvelous man stood up in a testimony meeting so touched by what he had heard as others had born their testimonies. With tears brimming, he said, "That which I have heard you say today, oh, I want this to be true. Oh, I hope this is true." That's the beginning of a testimony and faith—"Oh, I hope this message is true."

When the amen was said to that meeting, those elders I was seated next to went after him like a teenager for the phone. You know very well what they did with him! They gave him a Book of Mormon and a million Church pamphlets. They said, "Would you pray about this, would you read this Book of Mormon, would you get down on your knees and ask with sincerity and real intent?" Then they promised him that by the power of the Holy Ghost, the truth would be manifested to him.

Those actions of reading and praying are vitally important. The prophet Alma said, "Awake and arouse your faculties . . . experiment upon my words . . . if ye can no more than desire to believe, let this desire work in you." (Alma 32:27.) If we exercise a particle of faith, the Savior then responds, "I, the Lord, am bound when ye do what I say." (D&C 82:10.) If we put forth the proper actions, he will give proper confirmation, so that even though we don't see him, we will know he is there.

About six months after that experience, I was in that same area participating in a youth conference. I finished on Saturday and again went to church on Sunday before I returned home. While in church, I sensed that I was in a familiar setting.

I thought, "I've been here before." I couldn't figure out when, though. I started racking my brain, and it suddenly dawned on me that I had been there in that impressive testimony meeting.

After the sacrament meeting, I pulled a ward member aside and said, "I was here about six months ago and heard a man stand and bear his testimony as a nonmember." I shared the story, and a grin came onto the face of the person I was speaking to. "I was there as well," he said. "He's been baptized. He blesses our stake." Our nonmember visitor had tested the gospel principles. He had put forth proper actions and gained a confirmation of the truth.

Level 2 is when we say, "I believe this is true." We begin to act upon this belief, and our righteous actions increase. After the missionaries taught me in Japan, I hesitated to be baptized for several months. I had a good bishop who understood that there must be proper confirmations to increase testimony. He called me into his office one Sunday and challenged me, "Jack, you believe enough about this gospel; you ought to be baptized." I gulped. "You believe don't you?"

"Yes, I do, Bishop."

"You know enough! You get baptized!"

I quickly replied, "Okay, I'll get baptized."

Baptism is a great act of faith; it brings forth greater confirmation.

Some weeks later the bishop called me into his office again. "Jack, I've been checking our records; you haven't been paying your tithing."

When I was baptized I hadn't understood the principle as I should have. He took out the scriptures and taught me. When I somewhat understood, I said, "You want my money?"

"The Lord wants *his* money," he said. So I started paying my tithing.

Greater actions bring forth greater confirmations, which increase hope. A couple of weeks later, the bishop called me into his office again. "Jack, you don't have a job in the Church; where do you want to serve?"

"Anywhere but with the Scouts," I replied.

He called me to be the deacons quorum advisor and assistant cubmaster. Greater actions, in this case a supreme sacrifice, brought greater confirmations.

Before long, I was back in the bishop's office. "Jack," he said, "you haven't been paying your budget."

"What's budget?" I asked cautiously. He again took out the scriptures and taught me about offerings!

"You want more money?"

"The Lord wants more." I paid my budget, and my testimony grew.

Sometime later in the hallway by the sign-up sheet for the blood drive, the bishop said, "Jack, your name isn't on the blood drive!"

"You want my blood, too?"

"The Lord wants your blood."

I gave, and so did the Lord. I received greater confirmations.

Joseph Smith taught that a religion that does not require the sacrifice of all things never has the power to produce the faith necessary to lead us to salvation. Though we may never be asked to sacrifice all, we must be willing to.

Young people want to know the gospel is true; they want to know like their mother, father, bishop, and stake president. They, like you, may have also asked, "How do I know I'm coming to know?" or "Will I ever know it's true?" If you are troubled over that, remember what the Savior taught: "I, the Lord, am bound when ye do what I say." (D&C 82:10.) You don't have to worry about the confirmations coming; come they will. You need only to worry about taking care of your own actions.

President Joseph Fielding Smith spoke about those proper actions when he said, "I'm going to say something that maybe I cannot prove, but I believe this is true: that we have a great many members of this Church who have never received a manifestation through the Holy Ghost. Why? Because they have not made their lives conform to the truth. The Holy Ghost will not dwell in unclean tabernacles or disobedient tabernacles. The Holy Ghost will not dwell with that person who is unwilling to obey and keep his commandments. . . . That great gift of testimony comes through humility, faith, and obedience."

Where we might get into problems is where we take an action the Lord has prescribed and put question marks by it. Do I really need to live the Word of Wisdom? Is it really expected of me to live the law of chastity? Does the Lord really mean every young man should prepare himself for a mission? Remember, without the proper actions, confirmations are slow in coming.

As a person matures spiritually by righteous actions and those confirmations, he or she arrives at level three. That which was once "I hope this is true" becomes "I believe this is true" and then through diligent effort becomes "I know this is true." At this level, that of knowing, there is no such thing as blind faith. We may not understand how Heavenly Father will help us accomplish our goals or overcome our challenges, but we're assured of his help; we've seen it so many times before. Because of that assurance, we observe tremendous actions of sacrifice.

The following is from a letter from a student I taught in seminary, a good young man trying to live the gospel by serving a mission in Guatemala. Listen to his actions, his sacrifices, then the confirmations:

"Dear Brother Marshall: It's been a while since I last wrote, and for that I'm sorry. I want to let you know that I'm alive and doing fine. I can't say that it's been easy, because it hasn't. In the past two and a half months, I feel like I've been tested a little. It started when they had to operate on my toe and take the toenail off. That hurt! Just as my toe was getting better, one night our house was shot at, and three bullets came into our room. About two weeks after that, a dog bit me, and I had to get rabies shots. It wouldn't have been so bad if it had been one or two in the arm, but it was ten shots in the stomach. After about half of the series of shots, I received a good old Dear John letter from my girlfriend. This might sound like a lot of trials to you, but it doesn't matter to me. Through all this, I haven't forgotten who I am and why I am here. If anything, my testimony has grown from all this. I've learned what is important and what isn't. I know that God and his Son live, and I'll continue to preach the gospel faithfully. May God bless you. Elder Cisneros."

What knowledge from a twenty-year-old young man! When many of his peers in the world are trying to figure out what life is all about, this young man knows the gospel is true through sacrifice.

It is interesting to note that the Greek word for testimony or witness shares a common Greek root with our English word *martyr*. A martyr is one who sacrifices his life for a cause. Though we may never be required to give our life as a sacrifice for the cause of the gospel, in order to come to know the truth of the gospel we will be required to sacrifice time and talents and means for the cause of truth.

At level three, the confirmations become more and more direct and powerful. At this level, you will find great blessings, great administrations. Miracles are performed by those on this level. The confirmations at this level are powerful.

I had a marvelous sophomore student, a young woman who was conscientiously striving to live the gospel and doing a good job. She told me that while being baptized for the dead in the temple with her Mutual group, she saw a couple of kids who shouldn't have been in the temple. Mom and dad, youth advisors, and bishops are sometimes the last to know what problems their youth are involved in. But for the most part, peers are aware of the problems. The girl knew what these kids had been doing and that they had not been totally honest with their bishop. She was feeling a bit frustrated.

She told me she wasn't feeling judgmental, just confused: "I've really been trying to fight a good battle with temptation; they've compromised, but we were equal." They were in the temple doing the same thing, being baptized for the dead. While she was being baptized, she wondered if it made any difference to the people for whom the work was being performed. "I wonder if it counts. Does it count if an unworthy person is involved in an ordinance?" She reasoned further. "Of course it counts; that's what the 2nd Article of Faith is all about. We are punished for our own sins and not someone else's."

At the conclusion of her part in the baptism, even more confused and trying harder than ever to withold judgment, she turned to get out of the font. The ordinance worker, an elderly gentleman, held onto her elbow. She looked back at him. With a smile yet a piercing look, he said, "You're a good Latter-day Saint young lady, aren't you? You really love the gospel, don't you?"

Somewhat surprised by such an unusual question, she paused and pondered it. In that moment, assured by her loyal and valiant actions, she replied, "Yes, I really am trying to live the gospel; I am a good Latter-day Saint."

"I know," he replied, "I can tell. The Spirit bore witness of that to me as I baptized you." He gave her a little hug. "You just keep living the gospel and being a wonderful example."

"Brother Marshall," she said, "I floated out of the temple. Heavenly Father knew my thoughts and feelings in that moment while I was being baptized." She had been frustrated and confused, but the Lord had blessed her with clarity and understanding. Proper actions bring great confirmations of those unseen realities we hope for.

Eventually, through proper actions and confirmations, we arrive at a fourth level of faith and testimony. It is best described in D&C 93:1: "Verily, thus saith the Lord: It shall come to pass that every soul who forsaketh his sins and cometh unto me, and calleth on my name, and obeyeth my voice, and keepeth my commandments, shall see my face and know that I am." Notice the actions in those verses! A person at this level strives to live as Christ-like a life as possible.

Be patient with yourself. This is a process that takes a lifetime and sometimes more. The confirmation at this level is described in the end of the verse: those who strive to live a Christ-like life, the Lord says, "shall see my face and know that I am." In this life or the life to come, we can achieve a perfect knowledge, no longer a hope of unseen things.

That which was years ago, "I hope this is true," through proper action and confirmations becomes "I believe this is true." Continued effort and witnesses bring "I know this is true." Then, finally, through sacrifice and service and enduring to the end in this life or the hereafter, we come to know with a perfect knowledge that God is real and that his Son is the Christ. Arriving finally at our eternal destination of the ultimate confirmation, we become as they are, Gods and Goddesses.

This is a brief description of the pathway to testimony. Testimony means the principles have been tested and found true. That's what we're about. Much depends upon these tests, as Elder Robert L. Simpson put it so well: "May I suggest that this Church is not idly named. We are The Church of Jesus Christ of Latter-day Saints. These are the latter days; this is the final dispensation of time, and the programs of the Church are all moving toward a sort of finalization or culmination. There is an urgency as never before about what needs to be done; and be sure of this, what needs to be done will be done on schedule, we hope by those initially foreordained to the task. But just as surely as night follows day, if we choose not to accept our station, or if we grow weary along the way, placing less important things first, there will be substitutes raised to take our place, that the Lord's time-plan and ultimate purposes will not be thwarted. Youth of Zion, stand up and be counted, have the courage of your convictions, and whatever you do, don't allow someone else to be a substitute for you in the Kingdom of your Heavenly Father."

Jack S. Marshall is an institute director in Pasadena, California. He is a popular speaker at youth programs and has published articles in the New Era, *coauthored a book, and released two audio tapes of favorite talks. He and his wife, Liz, have five children.*

Chapter 9

Tactfully Tackling Today's Temptations

Todd Parker

A young man attending Brigham Young University had been out late one night with his girlfriend and consequently fell asleep during a lecture given by one of his professors the next day. In an attempt to embarrass the snoozing student, the professor woke him up by saying, "Jones, what do you think about that?"

Jones quickly awakened, but not knowing what the discussion was about he replied, "Professor, what do *you* think about that?" The professor responded, "I don't *think*, I *know*." Then, with a twinkle in his eye, Jones said, "I don't think I know either." Now, I don't think I know all there is to know about handling temptations. However, I have counseled with many young people about their problems, and I've spent some time studying the scriptures. I'd like to share with you some guidelines that the Lord has given us to help us deal with a world so filled with temptations—both open and subtle. I would like to list a few scriptures and try to liken them to us. (See 1 Nephi 19:23.)

The first scripture is Matthew 5:27-28: "Ye have heard that it was said by them of old time, Thou shalt not commit adultery: but I say unto you, That whosoever looketh on a woman to lust after her hath committed adultery with her already in his heart."

The commandment in verse 27 is, "Don't commit adultery." It's the third most serious sin on the all-time top-ten

94

sin list. (See Alma 39:5-6.) Christ's suggestion is to not even think unclean thoughts. (Matthew 5:28.) But in verses 29-30, he gives great council on how to avoid the sin. Because of the awkward wording, sometimes people skip past these verses.

Verses 29-30 read: "If thy right eye offend thee, pluck it out, and cast it from thee: for it is profitable for thee that one of thy members should perish, and not that thy whole body should be cast into hell. And if thy right hand offend thee, cut if off, and cast it from thee: for it is profitable for thee that one of thy members should perish, and not that thy whole body should be cast into hell."

What did the Lord mean when he said, "If thy right hand offend thee, cut if off, and cast it from thee"? The following is a newspaper article I clipped from the Mesa, Arizona Tribune several years ago: "An 18 year old man said he cut off his hand because he 'got in a fight with the devil,' then walked the streets with a Bible to preach the word of God, says the policeman who found him. Robert Huettl of Stonington, Conn., was in stable condition Tuesday night at Hartford Hospital following surgery to restore his right hand. A spokesman said it was too early to tell if the operation had been successful.

"Patrolman Frank Kania said he found Huettl Monday night as the youth was walking along Route 190, carrying a Bible under his arm and bleeding heavily. 'I asked him why he did it and he said, "If your right hand offends thee, cut if off and toss it away." ' Kania said Huetll made a tourniquet for his arm before cutting off the hand with a razor blade. An off-duty fireman who also stopped at the scene made a better tourniquet and called for another officer to retrieve the hand. It was found in a wastebasket in the room."

Is that the correct interpretation of Matthew 5:30? Can you imagine being the police officer called to retrieve the hand? "Officer Frimsley, would you please drop by the Motel 6 and pick up a hand?"

"Excuse me, sir, it that a hired hand?"

95

"No, it's in the wastebasket—just get it and bring it over here quick. Ten-four."

A close examination of the scripture reveals what Jesus actually intended to teach. A better definition of the word *offend* from the original Greek is "cause to stumble." In other words, if your eye is viewing something or your hand is tempted to touch something that would cause you to stumble spiritually, the Savior's advice is to get rid of the temptation. You should get away from it or not get near whatever it is that tempts you. He is suggesting that not only do we *not* do the sin, but also that we not even get near the temptation, let alone the sin.

Let's try to liken this scripture to us. Suppose you have a friend with a rifle collection. He allows you to come to his home and "sight in" his new rifles, which you have done several times. His basement is not very tidy, and you usually rummage through the mess to find something that you can use as a target on which to focus. In your searching, you find a stack of pornographic magazines. You are alone. No one will know if you look at them. Your eye is tempted to violate verse 28, "to looketh on a woman to lust," and your hand is tempted to touch something that would cause you to stumble spiritually. So what do you do? Do you stay there and work on the rifle, all the time fighting the temptation to look at the magazines? Or do you do what Jesus implies when he says you should "cast it from thee"—get totally away from the temptation? You would do better to leave. The writer of Proverbs wisely asks, "Can a man take fire in his bosom, and his clothes not be burned?" (Proverbs 6:27.) In other words, can you stay around a temptation and not have it affect you? No. You must remove yourself from the circumstance. Don't remain around temptation. Leave. Cut yourself off from it.

Joseph Smith gave us added insight to this verse when he supplemented the King James text with the words, "and a man's hand is his friend." (JST Matthew 18:9.) Jesus is saying that if your friend is the reason you are stumbling spiritually,

96

then cut him off. It is better that you enter into eternal life with one fewer friend than that you be cast into hell because of another's negative influence on your life. (See JST Matthew 18:9, footnote 9a in LDS Edition of the Bible.)

It is because friends sometimes cause us to stumble that President Spencer W. Kimball gave his advice about steady dating, French kissing, necking, and petting. When youth date steadily, they became close friends, become too familiar, and constantly find themselves in tempting situations where they have to resist physical attraction.

So to help you follow Jesus' counsel and remove yourself not only from committing the sin but also from even being in a position where you would be tempted to sin, President Kimball gives this advice: "When you get in the teenage years, your social associations should still be general acquaintance with both boys and girls. Any dating or pairing off in social contacts should be postponed until at least the age of 16 or older, and even then there should be much judgment used in selections and in the seriousness. . . . One can have all the blessings if he is in control and takes the experiences in proper turn: first some limited social get-acquainted contacts, then his mission, then his courting [going steady], then his temple marriage and his schooling and his family, then his life's work. In any other sequence he could run into difficulty." (*Ensign,* Feb. 1975, p. 4.)

President Kimball has also given counsel about French kissing. Before I quote President Kimball, however, I'd like to remind you of two things:

1. When a prophet speaks as a prophet, under the direction of the Spirit, his words are scripture. They are the mind, will, and voice of the Lord. (See D&C 68:2-4.) I therefore feel that these words are modern scripture to youth.

2. If you read these words and feel guilty, that is probably good—not good in the sense that you have been involved with French kissing, but good in the sense that your guilt is a spiritual signal. Nephi said, "the guilty taketh the truth to

be hard, for it cutteth them to the very center." (1 Nephi 6:2.)
Guilt is to the spirit what pain is to the body. If you are playing
basketball and twist an ankle, the physical pain gives you the
signal, "Stop! Don't do any more or you'll damage yourself
further!" If you read President Kimball's words and you feel
guilty, the message is "Stop! If you continue, you'll harm
yourself spiritually!"

President Kimball's counsel on French kissing is: "Kissing
has been prostituted and has been degenerated to develop
and express lust instead of affection, honor, and admiration.
To kiss in casual dating is asking for trouble. What do kisses
mean when given out like pretzels or robbed of sacredness?

"What is miscalled the [French] kiss is an abomination
and stirs passion that results in the eventual loss of virtue.
Even if timely courtship justifies a kiss, it should be a clean,
decent, sexless one, like the kiss between a mother and a son,
or a daughter and a father. If the [French] kiss with its passion
were eliminated from dating, there would be an immediate
upswing in chastity and honor, with fewer illegitimate babies,
fewer unwed mothers, fewer forced marriages, and fewer
unhappy souls. With the absence of the [French] kiss, necking
would be greatly reduced. Its younger sister, petting, would
be totally eliminated. Both are abominations of their own right
and kind. The persons who have indulged in such practices
need a purging to cleanse themselves and should seek assis-
tance from bishops to whom they should go and confess their
sins." (Mexico City Conference, Aug. 26, 1972.)

In summary, Jesus taught us to stay morally clean by
staying away from tempting situations, whether it be pornography, friends of evil influence, French kissing, or pre-
maturely going steady. He blessed us with a conscience so
we would feel guilt as a warning to help us avoid stumbling
spiritually.

The Apostle Peter wrote: "Sanctify the Lord God in your
hearts: and be ready always to give an answer to every man

that asketh you a reason of the hope that is in you with meekness and fear." (1 Peter 3:15.)

When Peter counsels us to have an answer ready, I like to interpret that as having a premeditated answer ready. It's hard sometimes to think or react under pressure. If we are wise, we will premeditate a potentially tempting situation, decide that we won't participate, and have a reply ready for whatever may be asked of us.

I learned that lesson from an unfortunate experience. I was dating a girl who had just moved into our school. A friend of mine, who was going steady with a girl, suggested that we double date. The date began at a recreation area where we played pool. Then my friend said, "I have a surprise for you." I said, "What is it?" He said, "You'll see. You'll love it."

We got in my car (actually it was my Dad's Volkswagen), and I started driving. He directed me to go down our town's main street, then up a mountain road, and off on a dirt road. I said, "Where are we going?" He said, "If I told you it would spoil the surprise." After we got to a secluded area, he said, "Okay, park here." I said, "What?" He said, "Park it, Parker." (That's my name, Todd Parker.) He leaned over the seat, turned off the ignition and pulled up the parking brake. He then proceeded to engage in premarital, heterosexual, succulent mastication of the obicularis oris—that's kissing.

I was shocked! I didn't know what to do. I had no answer ready, as Peter directs us. So what do you do? Do you turn around and say, "Stop that, you two! That's disgusting. It's carnal, sensual, and devilish!" Most of us wouldn't be so daring. So I just sat there, with those two making out in the back seat and my date staring at me. I thought "This is your big test, Parker. Are you going to act the way you've been taught or the way your best friend is acting?" I decided that I wouldn't do what he was doing, but I still had no answer— I didn't know what to say to get out of the situation. I started to talk. I talked about the North Star, the Big Dipper, and how to tell time by the stars the way I had learned in Boy Scouts. But it was still *so* uncomfortable. Then a thought occurred to me. I'd try something that had worked before in a similar situation.

I ran on the cross-country team. The coach didn't like us to stay out late on weekends, so the hardest workout of the week was always on Saturday morning. It punished those who had stayed out the latest on Friday night. I always wanted to get enough sleep so I wouldn't die during the Saturday morning workout. I also wanted to be with my friends. I didn't always want to be the one to say, "Take me home, I need to get my rest."

So I made a deal with my dad. I said, "Dad, I need your help. Can we make a deal that whenever I want to come home, I can make up a time and tell my friends you will get upset with me if I get in late?" He said, "If that is the way you want to handle it, it is okay with me." So when my friends and I were out late and I wanted to get to bed but I didn't want to look like a sissy, I'd say, "Oh, man, it's five to twelve! If I'm not home at midnight, my dad will *kill* me!" It made Dad the bad guy. But he didn't mind.

So, when I found myself parked with my friends, I thought, "I'll use dear old Dad to get out of this." I looked at my watch and said, "Holy mackerel—it's 11:40! If I don't have this car home by 12:00 Dad will kill me!" We left—Dad to the rescue. Now, I doubt that there is a concerned parent around who wouldn't be willing to be the "bad guy" to help their kids out of a tempting situation. Can you imagine asking your parents for such an arrangement and having them say, "No, you cannot make us be the bad guy—you stay out there and make out with that guy!"

Using your parents is only one alternative. Let me suggest some others. If a boy were to stop his car, turn off the ignition, and try his "clutch" on a girl, she should have an answer ready. I suggest quoting a scripture. She could say, "Wait! Do you know what it says in Colossians 2:21?" He may say,

"No, what does it say?" She could answer, "Touch not, taste not, handle not." The boy may then get her message. Another possible answer to improper advances is, "Listen, buddy, my body is a temple, not a visitor's center, and you don't have a recommend."

President Kimball suggests a more direct approach. He tells this story: "One young lady had an unpleasant experience. They were in the car, and the boy tried to take advantage of the girl, and she was courageous enough to say, 'Get over on your own side of the seat.' When he insisted on getting his arms around her, she said, 'You stop this car and let me get out, and if you don't, I'll knock out your teeth!' " (Mexico City Conference, Aug. 26, 1972.)

Not all of your temptations will be of this kind, however. A more common one is to have friends ask you to help them cheat in school. You may be taking a test and the teacher leaves the room. Your friend may say, "Hey, what is the answer to number six?" Most of us are afraid of looking too self-righteous as if to imply, "I'm so holy and righteous and you are so slothful and decadent. I refuse to give you the answer to number six." Remember Peter's advice to have an answer ready. You may say, "Use your brain—it's the small things in life that count."

You may have someone tempt you with a cigarette or drugs by saying, "Would you like one of these?" You may say, "Sure, I'd love one!" Then take the cigarette, shred it into pieces, and say, "That was great! May I have another one?" His reply may be, "Don't give this guy anything—he's weird."

I have only listed a few ideas about avoiding temptations. There are undoubtedly many more that you can think of. I honestly believe that if you do at least these basic things, Satan's attempts to control you will be thwarted. In summary they are:

1. Remove yourself from tempting people and situations.

2. Have answers ready in your mind for difficult situations that might arise.

It is my sincere prayer that these suggestions will help you avoid temptations in these latter days.

Todd Parker is an institute instructor at the University of Arizona. He enjoys sports and has been a pole vaulter, a gymnast, and a distance runner. In college, he broke his neck in a pole-vaulting accident, but the vertebrae were fused and he still pole vaults on occasion. He and his wife, Debra, have six children. They live in Tucson, Arizona.

Chapter 10

Self-Portraits:
Picturing Your Best Self

Kim M. Peterson

I remember hurrying home from sixth grade one Friday afternoon to make sure that my football uniform was washed and ready to wear. As the left cornerback and defensive captain of the "midget" little-league football team, I had to look good for the pictures being taken that day. Carefully I dressed, making sure that my uniform and equipment were properly assembled before I rushed off to practice.

One by one, the players and coaches arrived at the familiar practice field. In spite of the next day's impending game, warmups, calisthenics, and scrimmaging were replaced by combing hair, adjusting shoulder pads, and cleaning helmets (all of which we considered beneath our dignity as the second-place "midget" team in our league). One by one, we approached the photographer. While standing in line, we practiced holding our faces in serious positions like the football players we had seen on television. Facial expression was the key to a good picture. We had to look like football was fun, but not like we were enjoying it; we had to appear handsome but naturally tough.

The boy in front of me finished, and my turn came. With shoulders flexed, stomach in, and helmet under my arm, I tried to walk as if I were fourteen instead of eleven. I knelt in the appropriate spot and assumed my practiced expression. As the photographer prepared to shoot the picture, he tried to make me smile. I fought hard not to smile, and instead of looking naturally tough, I looked unnaturally awkward; instead of looking like I was having fun, I looked like I was holding an over-sized jawbreaker in my mouth; instead of looking handsome, I looked like a "geek." I really hate that picture and go to great lengths not to show it to anyone.

Cameras do not lie. In spite of all the techniques a photographer employs, the film can only record the light that comes through the lens. The photographer has the capacity to focus through the lens. When the lens is focused on close objects, however, objects in the distance are not clear. Conversely, when a lens is focused on objects in the distance, those nearby are unrecognizable. This simple definition of "depth of field" illustrates a profound principle. If you were going to take a self-portrait, where would you focus? How do you picture the best of you?

One obvious answer to the question is that you could focus on your body. How do you like your body? As a society, we are obsessed with the way we look (or the way we don't look). Most of us have received a yearbook on yearbook day. When you finally get the book, which picture do you look for first? Don't you look for your own first? When you find your portrait, the one by which everyone will remember you, do you look for what is right or what is wrong with the picture? As you walk into school, do you check yourself in the reflection of the door? Are you looking for what is right, or are you looking for what is wrong? Mirrors lie; they show us only what is wrong. How many of us would like to find a mirror with a better view?

Physically, most of us are so uncomfortable that we are constantly disguising ourselves. Why do girls wear make-up? They wear make-up to make up for what they are not. Some of us disguise ourselves with clothes. Those who think they are too fat have learned that vertical stripes make the wearer look skinnier; and those who think they are too skinny have learned that horizontal stripes make the wearer look bigger. I remember taking a weight-lifting class with a goal of developing muscles so large they would split my shirt. After some effort and a lot of frustration, I put on a shirt one size too small; splitting that one was easy.

Disguises can be dangerous. Shakespeare wrote a play centering on disguises. In *Twelfth Night*, Viola is shipwrecked on an island. Imagine what she looks like when she crawls onto the shore; better yet, imagine how she feels when the prince sees her. Viola immediately falls in love with the prince and formulates a plan for the two of them to meet: She dresses up like a boy, cuts her hair, and applies for a job as the prince's pageboy. Viola gets the job but doesn't anticipate being employed to court the prince's sweetheart, Olivia.

With ring in hand, Viola goes to court Olivia for the prince. Just to complicate matters, Olivia does not fall in love with the prince but with his pageboy/girl. So now the girl dressed like a boy is in love with the prince; a girl is in love with the girl who is in love with the prince. The prince, however, is in love with the girl who is in love with the girl who is in love with him. Viola walks out of the encounter saying, "I've got a headache, and its got Excedrin written all over it." Actually, she says: "Fortune forbid my outside have not charm'd her [Olivia]! She made good view of me; indeed, so much, that methought her eyes had lost her tongue, for she did speak in starts distractedly. She loves me, sure; the cunning of her passion invites me in this churlish messenger. None of my lord's ring! why, he sent her none. I am the man: if it be so, as 'tis, poor lady, she were better love a dream. *Disguise, I see, thou art a wickedness,* wherein the pregnant enemy does much. How easy is it for the proper-false in women's waxen hearts to set their forms! Alas, our frailty is the cause, not we! *For such as we are made of, such we be.* How will this fadge? my master loves her dearly; and I, poor monster, fond as much on him; and she, mistaken, seems to dote on me. What will become of this? As I am man, my state is desperate for my master's love; as I am woman,—now alas the day!—what thriftless sighs shall poor Olivia breathe? *O time! thou must untangle this, not I; it is too hard a knot for me to untie."* (Act 2, scene 2.)

There are at least three profound lessons to be learned from Viola's masquerade. First, disguises are lies; lies always come back to the liar. The next time you are attempting to disguise yourself, ask this question: Do you want people to like you for what you aren't or for what you are?

Secondly, "Such as we are made of, such we be." Genesis 1:26–27 suggests that we are made "in the image of God." If we are made in the image of God, our physical selves should lead our thoughts to him whose image we resemble.

Lastly, time will tell. If we persist in hiding, disguising, and running from ourselves, time will untangle the knots we have tied. In other words, when we are finished with disguises and are caught in our lies, we will return to being ourselves once again.

We must realize that as we focus on our physical selves, many other important things are out of focus. Indeed, the physical depth of field is not very deep at all.

What if we were to focus on accomplishments as a source of self-esteem? The word "best" can apply only to one person at a time. Are you the best at anything? While you might be good at drawing, singing, swimming, or running, there is a good chance that someone is more artistic, has a clearer voice, has a smoother stroke or quicker gait than you do. Being best is nice. Is being good any consolation?

As a teenager in high school, I learned an important lesson about accomplishments. After trying and failing at basketball, football, and track, I decided to play chess (you didn't have to try out for the chess team.) I played third on the team for the whole year. I never became the best chess player of my school, but I loved to ski.

We had an exceptional ski team at our high school. I never had the courage to try out for that team, but none of the skiers played chess. The two chess players in front of me didn't ski.

Would it be safe to say that I was the best skiing chess player at my high school?

Each of us is best at one thing: being ourselves. We don't necessarily have to be the best at one thing in order to be proud of the many things at which we have become skilled. When we focus on accomplishments as a source of esteem, we may lose focus of what we have done in light of what we haven't done. Indeed, the very fact that we have bodies suggests that we accomplished one great feat: we kept our first estate.

What kind of portrait would we see if we focused on friends as a source of esteem? The social self depends upon the opinion of other people. If, however, your friends depend on you as the source of their self-esteem while you use them as the source of your self-esteem, a real dilemma is started. Just as you can't draw water from an empty well or eat from an empty plate, you can't derive esteem from someone who hasn't got it.

Frequently, friends attempt to increase their self-esteem by putting each other down. Consider how many times you have been cut down in the last twenty-four hours. Not only did your friends' esteem fail to increase as a result of cutting you down, but if you were the supposed source of their esteem, then your friends diminished their own esteem in the process.

Some teenagers would like to believe that dating is a source of esteem. Many teenagers, however, are also terrified of being turned down for a date. Just for a moment, rate yourself from one to ten (the game changes when it is you rating you). Suppose that you are an eight. You desperately want to go out with a ten, but you wouldn't dream of going with a six. In other words, you want the ten to do for you what you won't do for the six. It probably won't happen. If dating were not your source of esteem, you would be comfortable asking anyone for a date simply because it would not matter if anyone turned you down. Conversely, it would not matter if you dated someone less popular than you because it would not matter what other people said. Focusing on friends as a source of self-esteem will result only in having the friends in focus and the self out of focus.

The only scriptures on Christ's youth are found in the Gospel of Luke, chapter 2. Christ's adolescence is summarized with these words: "Jesus increased in wisdom and stature, and in favour with God and man." (Luke 2:52.) The Son of God grew mentally, physically, spiritually, and socially. We have considered our physical selves, our accomplishments (mental selves), and our friends; what if we focused on our spirits as a source of esteem?

One day, I was taking a picture of a flower. With my camera set, I attempted to focus on the delicate petals, stem, and leaves of the plant. As I looked through the lens, an intriguing pattern revealed itself in the background. Turning my lens, I shifted my focus from the flower at my feet to the majestic canyon beyond. I had nearly missed the incredible view in front of my face because I was focusing at something near my feet. I took the picture and looked at the distance indicator on my lens. Interestingly enough, my lens was turned to the infinity mark. What does infinity mean? Isn't it profound that with a lens set for infinity, miles of canyon were in focus, but with the lens set for two feet, only the flower was in focus?

Let me introduce you to your spirit. Without it, you would be dead—literally. Your spiritual parents are the same as mine. That makes us brothers and sisters; we're related. Just as your physical body resembles your mom and dad, your spirit resembles its parents. The more familiar you are with your spirit, the more familiar you will be with your heavenly parents. I even know what kind of spiritual food you like (see 2 Nephi 32:3), what kind of clothes you wear (see D&C 27:15–18), and where you would like to live (see John 14:2). Your spirit is the only real you, and the only reliable source of esteem.

The word *esteem* is confusing. The dictionary suggests that esteem means: "to hold in high regard; to prize dearly." (*Webster's Student's Dictionary* [New York City: American Book Co., 1959], p. 283.) How important is it that we esteem ourselves? Indeed, the scriptures suggest that we should not esteem ourselves better than others. In Philippians 2:3, we find these words: "In lowliness of mind let each esteem other better than themselves." God, however, esteems all flesh as one. (See 1 Nephi 17:35.) When you focus on eternity, your spirit testifies that your body is formed in the image of God, that your mind should be centered on him, and that your friends should be led by him.

Your spirit is eternal, your spirit is the child of God, and your spirit responds to truth. When your spirit is in focus, eternity is in focus, and your true value is revealed. "Remember the worth of souls is great in the sight of God." (D&C 18:10.) "I have said, Ye are gods; and all of you are children of the most High." (Psalm 82:6.) In order to picture your best self, focus on infinity.

Kim M. Peterson is a seminary instructor at Skyline High in Salt Lake City, Utah. He loves to ski and works as training director at Brighton ski school. He also enjoys golf, photography, and cooking "Eastern dishes." He and his wife, Terri, have two children.

Chapter 11

Why Are Boys So Dumb?
Some Insights on Dating

Dave Thomas

I am concerned about something that's been bothering me for some time. It bothers me because I see lots of unnecessary frustration in the eyes of people that I truly care for. Primarily, I see that frustration in the eyes of girls. But I think there's something we can do about it. I'd like to talk to you about some possible reasons why girls are so frustrated. There's only one real reason, and the reason is simple—it's boys! You need to understand why boys are so frustrating: Boys are retarded. When we say, "Boys are retarded," what we're saying is, "Boys are slower"—boys are slower than girls.

Girls are taught from tiny munchkinhood how to be women. They're taught how to walk, how to sit, how to do their hair and makeup. Everything is done with one primary objective—to teach girls how to be desirable so that they can attract boys. So girls come fully equipped, fully prepared, fully taught to do their job as girls.

But what do we tell the boys? Nothing. We keep the boys completely in the dark, and the reason is that if the boys knew anything, they'd be dangerous.

While girls are being taught how to sit, walk, and dance, boys are simply told to take their ball and go play in the street. The result is that you have girls working, working, working to attract the boys, and the boys just stand around in small groups saying, "What is she doing?" "I don't know. You want to go get something to eat?" And they walk off and leave the girl standing in full desirability. She looks absolutely gorgeous. But the guys just wander off. The girl's left there, and who does she blame? Does she blame the retarded boys? No, she blames herself.

Let me tell you something about girls that you need to know. Girls go to the mirror and check everything out, and they have a list. One side of the list is the things that are good about them, and the other side is the things that are bad. Would you like to guess which side is the longest? It's always the bad things. The negative side of the list goes on and on and on.

Now what I want to know is, where do girls get this stuff? Where do they get the authority to judge whether their ankles are good or bad? And one of the things I find interesting about girls is that they worry about things boys would never worry about. They come up to you all frantic and say, "I can't remember which is in, attached or unattached ear lobes." Or they say, "Are my elbows weird? Are the backs of my knees supposed to look like this? Are my ankles fat?" Boys would never worry about such things, but girls do. "My toes are weird. I know my toes are weird. These are not normal toes." And girls will figure all these bad things out, and there's virtually no way you can get them to change their minds. "This is good and that is bad; don't argue with me." So you've got a girl with a long list of faults, and she's absolutely convinced she's right.

Have you ever been seasoned—found out whether you were a summer, winter, spring, or mud? My wife went out and got seasoned. I can't remember what she was; I think she was an autumn. One of the things she had to do was go up to a complete stranger and ask him to pick out three adjectives that best described his first impression of her. My wife's a courageous woman, but I had never before seen her so frightened. She put it off for weeks until finally the seasoning people said, "If you don't do this assignment, we won't tell you which season you are." She became so frightened by that pressure that she started looking for friendly strangers. Now, fortunately, I had a new friend she had never met, so he was a stranger to her but a friend to me. She thought, "He's friendly to Dave, so maybe he will be kind to me." So she went to him and asked him to pick out the three adjectives. The first was "vivacious." The second was "capable." And the third was "attractive." Of course she got positive feedback—and just by asking!

Many girls never get any positive feedback, so without ever asking someone else, they make major decisions about their appearance. I think that's unkind and unfair. Now I grant you, boys are retarded. Are boys going to rush right up and say, "You're the most beautiful woman I've ever met"? No. The result is a whole bunch of girls who are frustrated because boys are retarded.

Girls are desperate. Now what are girls desperate for? If you talk to teenage boys, they're very quick with the answer: "Girls are desperate for us." Girls aren't desperate for boys as much as they are desperate for the confirmation that boys can give, the assurance that boys can give. Boys can say something nice to a girl and the girl will believe it. If your father says, "You're the most beautiful girl I know," your response is, "What do you know?" If your bishop says, "You sure look pretty today," you look at him and say, "God pays you to say those things." There's something in the girl's mind that will resist with a vengeance anything positive that's said to her. If you don't believe me, say something nice to a girl. She will argue with you. You say, "Your hair looks beautiful," and she says, "It does not." "No, honestly, your hair looks gorgeous." "I haven't washed it for weeks." And she will go on like that forever.

Why do girls do that? It's simple—girls are desperate. What are they desperate for? The assurances and compliments that girls don't get enough of. When you are taught from babyhood that your primary purpose in life is to be gorgeous, do you need to hear that you're gorgeous now and then? Of course you do, and the problem is that girls are fairly dependent on retarded boys to give them that information.

So how long has it been since somebody gave you that kind of information? A long time, and what is sad is that girls are so eager to get positive feedback that they put boys in a very awkward position called a "double bind." The double bind is shaped like a T. If you put a white rat into a maze and run him all over the place, eventually he comes to a little blocked area shaped like a T. He starts at the bottom of the T and then runs up to the top where the T crosses. Then he thinks, "I can go right or I can go left." What the poor thing doesn't know is that on the right side of the T is a metal plate charged with about twelve thousand volts of electricity. So he says, "I'll go right." When he does, he gets the twelve thousand volts in his little paws. He dances around thinking, "This must be wrong." So he goes back to the center of the T and thinks, "I'll go left." What he doesn't know is that there's another metal plate with twelve thousand volts over there, so he dances around on that side and thinks, "This must be wrong." Then he returns to the center of the T and says to himself, "I don't have a choice. There's no way I can win." So a double bind is a no-win situation. There's virtually no way a young man can make the right choice about what young women want.

Let me give you an example of what I mean. When a girl goes out on a date the boy is expected to show interest in the girl, but if he makes a play he gets zapped on the right! If he decides to go left and doesn't try anything, he's zapped on the left! So the boy sits in the center thinking, "What does she want from me?" Is it appropriate for guys to make a move? No. Then why do we get everything so confused? I think it's because boys are retarded and girls are desperate, and I'd like to see if we can simplify the problem.

First, are you aware that boys and girls talk different languages? This is how a boy would describe a date: "Good time, picked up girl in car, took her to show, bought her a hamburger after show, took her home, nice time, thank you." If you blink, you'll miss the story. Boys like to get the story over with and go get something to eat. Boys have places to go and people to see. They're not into talking like girls are. Girls love to talk. Girls will talk all the way to school, all day at school, all the way home on the bus. When they get home, they rush into the house, call a friend on the phone, and talk all night.

This is how the girl would describe the date: "It was a warm summer evening. A gentle breeze was blowing across the lake, and I sensed that this would be an evening of magic. I stood in front of my wardrobe wondering whether I should go with the peach ensemble, which highlights the color of my hair, or the blue ensemble, which brings out the color of my eyes. I realized to my amazement that my date was down in the living room and I, . . . " Well, we can't go into that right now, because, as you can see, she's still deciding what to wear. What I want you to understand is that if we're lucky, the girl will finish the story in maybe two and a half days. The story will go on and on, and the girls who are listening to the story will gather around the girl, kind of like boys gather around a campfire to roast marshmallows, and they toast their psyches on this story. I don't know what they're getting out of it, but they're getting something, because periodically they'll ask questions to keep the story going.

Why do we go on dates? The first reason is to have fun. Fun means that something is almost as good to remember as it was to do. Remember Disneyland? That's fun. You can't wait to go back and do that again. That's what fun is like. You not only enjoy remembering it, but you can't wait to do it again. Fun is something that has no regret in it, no remorse, no shame. Fun is pure, unadulterated, righteous pleasure, and most of us don't get enough of it. When you're young, you have so many other things in your head that sometimes you miss the fun.

Another reason for dating is to develop social skills. This basically means that if you're a girl and you're out with a guy, you don't become an idiot. You can sit with him and carry on a full conversation; you have complete thoughts, and there are all sorts of wonderful things going on in your brain that are not interrupted by the fact that you're with a boy. You're in control. If you're a boy and you have social skills, when you're with a girl you don't drool. You're in control. You know how to talk to her, you're comfortable with her. That's what social skills are, and what is really sad is that too many people don't do enough dating to develop those social skills. As a result, they spend the rest of their lives being uncomfortable with the opposite sex. Take advantage of this opportunity to develop social skills and to be comfortable with other people.

The Church organizes activities so you can have opportunities to get together, have fun, and develop social skills. The problem is, too many teenagers want to put a third item on the list—love. Too many teenagers think they're supposed to date for love. But love doesn't really need a lot of help; love will generally take care of itself. Love when you're fourteen is a headache. Love when you're fifteen is a headache. Until you've got your act together and you know who you are (if you're a boy, this will generally be when you're back from your mission), love can be a bother. So you shouldn't be rushing out trying to find love right now.

You'd be amazed at how many girls are convinced that if they have a boyfriend, all their problems will go away. But what do you find when you have a boyfriend? More problems. The fact is that you need to have not *a* boyfriend but rather *grundles* of boyfriends. Then you have lots of opportunities to develop social skills by meeting lots of different people. The worst form of social retardation in the world today is something called "going steady." You know what that means? That means you tie yourself up with one person exclusively. But when you do that, how many people do you really get to know? Just one.

Do you think cottage cheese is better than shrimp? Better

115

than steak? Probably not. Is anything wrong with cottage cheese? No, it's a fine food. But should you eat cottage cheese exclusively? No, you need to try other foods so you can find out what you really like. Going steady is like locking yourself into cottage cheese, and you spend three years of your life eating nothing but cottage cheese, never knowing that steak and chicken and shrimp and all those other wonderful things are out there. You've never tried pizza. Can you imagine? You've missed pizza because you were locked into cottage cheese.

If you're dating for fun and developing social skills, does it matter if you're a girl and a boy is shorter than you? No, because you're dating for fun and social skills. If you're dating for fun and social skills, does he have to be the most romantic, most dynamic, most magnificent man you've ever seen in your life? No, because that's not the agenda yet, is it? The agenda is to have fun and develop social skills. Doesn't this free you up a little bit? If you're dating for fun and social skills, do all your girlfriends have to like you? No. If you make these two things the priorities of your dating, you can have a lot of wonderful times and a lot of opportunities to date that you might not have if you were only dating the man of your dreams. It's the same for boys. If you're dating for fun and social skills, she doesn't have to ring your chimes. She can just be a good friend.

Girls see the world in a way boys will never see it. If you are a boy and you don't learn to see the world through a girl's eyes, you will never see it. They see so much more of it than boys do. You've got to have lots of girlfriends, not *a* girlfriend, but *lots* of girlfriends you can talk to and share with and get to understand. You can begin to get a handle on all this wonderful world by seeing it through the eyes of other people. You've got to learn how to respond to a girl's mind. That takes social skills, and you have to have them.

Girls often wonder why boys don't ask them out. The main reason is money—lack of money gets in the way. Another reason boys don't come around is that they don't have a car. Or, more specifically, they don't have the *right* set of wheels. Another reason boys don't ask girls out is they lack those social skills we were talking about. They don't know how to go through the motions of doing what needs to be done to take you out. They'd love to go out with you, but they don't know how to ask or how to behave. They'd love to go out with you, but they don't know the ups and downs of how it's done. So, they worship from afar, and the girls never know.

Girls need to be aware that most boys are not perverted, wicked people. They're wholesome and clean. I believe that guys can actually be more romantic than girls if they are given the opportunity. I also believe there are girls who are starring in male fantasies and don't even know it. If you're a girl, some guy at a distance may be dreaming about you, thinking about you, fantasizing about the possibility of winning your hand. He's dreaming a beautiful story, and you don't even know you're in it! If you could see the story as it's played in his mind, you would be very complimented.

Imagine a beautiful sunset with pink, fleecy clouds. Imagine yourself in a full-length dress, all lacy and gorgeous. You are going to high school. On your way, a tyrannosaurus rex comes out of the forest. He picks you up and is about to drag you into the bushes and have you for dinner. Suddenly from out of nowhere comes the boy having the fantasy. He attacks that tyrannosaurus rex—he punches it in the gut, hits it in the nose, and scares it away. Maybe then, he thinks, you will go out for root beer with him.

One of your great frustrations may be that you are fourteen or fifteen and want to date, but the Church and your family say you can't date until you're sixteen. You get so angry you want to have a bloody nose over it, right? Because Sylvia dates, and Frances dates, and Fred dates, but you can't. The whole world dates, but not you. I want to bear my witness to you that President Spencer W. Kimball was right in taking

117

that position. I want you to know that from the depth of my heart I am completely convinced that President Kimball knew what he was doing in encouraging people to wait until they are sixteen to date. I know that, because for three years I taught ninth grade. And I got to know what fourteen- and fifteen-year-old kids are like. And I want you to know that's not the time to be dating. At that age, you're just starting to get your agenda together, you're just starting to figure things out, and, if anything, you're too enthusiastic.

When you look at this list of things that keep boys from dating you, please be aware that none of those reasons has anything to do with your desirability. What it has to do with is the maturity and the availability and the readiness of the boys. And if you will be patient, the time will come when the boys will be everything you want them to be. They'll catch up with you. Please don't get so frustrated that you grovel or beg for their attention. If you have to beat the boy into submission to get the assurance that you're desirable and beautiful, does it really count? Isn't it much nicer just to play it cool and wait for him to move? Then you know that he's doing it for himself. He isn't doing it because you pushed him into it.

I believe that every girl has an inalienable right to know she's beautiful. I think it's written in the constitution: "We believe that women should know they're beautiful." But if you push it too hard, you destroy that experience for yourself. Look around you, look at the guys. They're eager. They're excited. They're not moving quite as fast as you'd like them to, but they're having the feelings, and they're responding to you almost the way you'd like them to. They're just doing it quietly, on the inside. I honestly believe that if girls knew how hard it was to be a boy, they would stop boys in the hall, throw their arms around them, pat them on the back, and say, "There, there, Mother understands." But is it easy to be a girl? There are lots of difficulties in being a girl also.

Please remember that boys are slow. They're going to

catch up, but they're slow. Remember that girls are desperate. They're not desperate for physical contact; they're desperate for an opportunity to hear that they're beautiful, lovely, desirable, attractive. One of the most powerful things a boy could learn is how to tell a girl something nice in such a way that she would believe it. You need to watch a girl long enough to know what she's confident in. Then when you tell her something, she really is sure that you know what you're talking about. You can help her stretch her scope of herself.

I want you to understand we're in this thing together as brothers and sisters. Should any sister of ours be desperate? No. Should any brother of ours be retarded? No. We should love and lift and take care of one another. What I'd like to recommend is that you look out for your brothers and sisters in such a way that we can grow through this experience of maturing and developing our social skills and having fun.

Dave Thomas is a seminary instructor at Brighton High in Utah. He also teaches business communications at the University of Phoenix at Salt Lake City. He has his own company called Life Navigators, and he is the author of the book There Are No Dragons Out There. *He and his wife, Paula, have six children.*

Chapter 12

Taking the Dead
out of Dedication

Brad Wilcox

"Let's split up." If the words had been coming from a girlfriend or a wife, I'd have been concerned, but since they were only coming from a mission companion, I wasn't too worried.

I had been on my mission about four months when the whole town of Vallenar, where I was working, stopped working and crammed into the local cemetery. It was a national holiday to honor the dead.

Children carried bundles of purple and yellow wildflowers. Mothers and fathers brought buckets of water, rags, and candles to clean and adorn the markers on the graves of their loved ones.

My companion, Elder Petersen, and I had worked for a week preparing a booth at the cemetery entrance where we could answer questions about death and let people know about eternal families. When the day came, Elder Petersen decided we could cover more territory if we split up with some local companions. "You take one of the priests and I'll go with Hermano Delgado," he said. "We'll meet back here at noon."

Obediently I left the booth and began roaming with a sixteen-year-old companion, who obediently left his friends and began roaming with me. Then, while looking the other way, we both roamed headlong into a Catholic nun coming around the corner of a mausoleum. The pamphlets we were

120

holding and the lilies she was carrying combined in the air like a fireworks display. After the crowd-shocking spectacle was over, I knelt in embarrassment and quickly began gathering the sister's flowers. She knelt beside me picking up our scattered pamphlets.

"I've always seen you Mormon elders around," she said in Spanish, "but I've never talked to one before."

"Well, ah . . . " I stammered. "I've always seen Catholic nuns around, but I've never talked to one before either."

When the lilies were salvaged, I helped the sister up. "I'm sure sorry," I said politely.

"Don't worry," she responded even more politely.

"Where are you from?" I inquired.

"Italy," she responded. "And you?"

"Utah." We both smiled. "I've only been here two months," I added.

"You must miss your family very much." The sister began arranging the flowers in her hands.

"I do," I assured her.

"I know how it feels," she said wistfully. "I haven't seen my family for over twenty years now."

"Twenty years?" I almost dropped my pamphlets again. Twenty years without seeing home. Twenty years without seeing her family! I was going crazy after only a few months of being away from mine.

The sister began to gather her flowers and skirts to leave. I ached for her. "God bless you," she said, extending her hand.

"Gracias, Hermana." I watched her walk away.

"Aren't nuns stupid?" my young companion blurted. "They don't even get married, and they wear those hot, old robes. They're too dedicated."

"Listen," I stopped him. The tone of my voice almost laid him into one of the open graves nearby. "There's nothing wrong with that sister's dedication. I admire it. I envy it. I wish more members of our Church had it."

"But . . . " he tried to defend himself.

I cut him off. "There may be some faults with what she's dedicated to, but nothing's wrong with her dedication. Got that?"

When God sent messengers to Paul or Alma the Younger, he did not condemn their dedication. I don't suppose God was too thrilled about what they were dedicated to at the time, but he never condemned their dedication. Instead, he wanted Paul and Alma to take the same energy and effort and channel them to righteous purposes. I think God didn't mind them working like the devil—he just didn't want them working for the devil.

I am told that most avalanche victims become disoriented and, trying to save themselves, actually dig in the wrong direction. It is not because they can't dig themselves out, but rather because the snow is all around them, they don't know which way to go. As we get buried in a multitude of causes requiring our dedication—school, job, arts, athletics, recreation, clubs, church, charities, and even tracting out the graveyard at Vallenar, Chile—we are often left disoriented. When we feel buried, the question is not "Should we dig?" Most of us agree that we should. Rather, the question is "Which way should we dig?" When we are surrounded by an avalanche, effort and dedication are not nearly as important as direction.

"If you're ever buried in snow," a skier friend tells me, "clear an area and spit. The gravity will draw the liquid downward, letting you know which way is up." Under a snowslide of causes, we too need to stop now and then, clear an area, and find our direction. We must ask ourselves, "Are these purposes worth our dedication? Do these causes merit our consecration? Are they helping us gain the experiences we were sent here to gain and become the people we need to become?" Then, as powerfully and consistently as gravity, the force of the Spirit will help us point ourselves upward so we can start digging toward life.

"Brad." Twelve-year-old Tiffany called my name and

walked down the aisle of the bus to where I was sitting. "Will you answer an important question?" she asked. For a girl who usually traveled like a space shuttle, Tiff was unusually somber. Trailing behind her came all the kids in the touring group: Dave, Russell, Paul, and Georgia, their eyes filled with grown-up seriousness.

"I'll try," I said, inviting them to sit. I was in the middle of writing a sentence that was in the middle of a paragraph that was in the middle of some thought that I knew I'd forget, but I gathered these chicks together as best I could. Most father hens don't have to worry about cramped bus seats and suitcases.

Tiffany began, "What if you repent of something bad . . . "

"Like lying?" Dave interrupted.

"Not that we lied," Tiffany assured me. But if someone did . . . "

I had no chalkboard, visual aids, charts, or even a lesson manual, but I had a class ready to learn, so Sunday School was in session. The question turned to temples and recommend interviews. Then we went to paradise and the spirit prison and finally ended our tour in the celestial kingdom. What a bus ride!

"But it's hard to be good all the time," Tiffany said rebelliously.

"But," I said, touching her arm, "it's worth it."

"Brad, I know this girl in another church, and they don't have to do half the stuff we do—I mean, I know our church is true, but she says hers is, and . . . " She paused as though she wished she had never said anything.

"And what?" I prodded.

"Well, what if she's right and we're wrong?"

It is good to see kids think. It was fun to see these future missionaries pondering past the swimming pools and hamburgers that usually filled their minds.

"If your friend is right," I told Tiffany, "you are spending a lot of good time and talent for the wrong cause. If we are right, your friend had better join up quickly so her work and efforts aren't dedicated to something that's temporary — something that's not going to last."

"To bring to pass the immortality and eternal life of man" (Moses 1:39) is not just a cause — something to work on between saving whales, studying advanced placement English, and helping with political campaigns — it is *the* cause. Our eternal lives and the lives of each of our brothers and sisters are not just another purpose. They are *the* purpose.

Different interests and talents keep us all digging constantly up through personal mountains. The time I spend writing a book, for example, is worth the effort for me but might be time wasted for Guppy Shmar, who likes football, stamp collecting, or putting car engines together. That's the beauty of free agency. We can choose which objectives we want to dig for. However, when the avalanche of revealed truth hits Guppy, Tiffany, me, or whomever, we must understand that some things are worth everyone's shoveling. Freedom is for everyone. Baptism is for everyone. The Word of Wisdom and the law of chastity are for everyone. A mission is for every young man. Whether we accept these truths and dedicate ourselves to them is up to us, but whether they are best for us and worth our sacrifices has already been decided.

"Well, that's what you think," a man I used to visit would tell me.

"You believe what you want, and I'll believe what I want. We're all entitled to our own opinions." I accept that. But if I were being tried by a jury that was to proclaim me guilty or innocent of something, I hope the jury would search out the truth. I hope they would free me or convict me because they *knew* one way or the other and not just because they were entitled to their own opinions. "Getting along" comes through understanding each other's opinions. Salvation comes through understanding truth.

Elder Neal A. Maxwell has said, "God's doctrines were

given to bring men closer to him. Modifications attempted by men may seem to bring them closer to each other, but they will be more and more distant from their Father in heaven! (*Things As They Really Are* [Salt Lake City: Deseret Book Company, 1978], p. 49.)

"So how can I know for sure what's true?" Tiffany asked.

An important question, for if Brad Wilcox and Tiffany are going to lose their whole lives, as the scriptures instruct, then they want to lose them in the cause that ensures that they will find them again. (See Matthew 16:24-25.)

Over and over we are counseled in the scriptures to take up our crosses. (D&C 23:6; 56:2; 112:14.) But I want to carry the crosses that will leave me toughened and stronger for the experience—not the ones that will leave me with nothing but splinters. One of my favorite questions to ask the young people I work with is, "What is the best thing about the Church?" After they answer, I ask, "What is the hardest thing about being LDS?" Invariably, I am flooded with a list: early morning seminary, the Word of Wisdom, keeping the Sabbath day, the strict moral code, explaining to friends why we don't see R-rated movies, having to go on a mission, service projects, group dating, paying tithing, not enough boys at stake dances, too many boys at stake dances, having to wear a tie to church—the list goes on and on. One young man said, "The hardest thing is that everyone else thinks we are so weird."

These are definitely crosses to bear—heavy crosses that, as Elder Neal A. Maxwell writes, "we could scarcely endure . . . without knowing the truth." (*Things As They Really Are*, p. 12.)

President Gordon B. Hinckley said, "Self-discipline . . . virtue . . . obedience to commandments . . . these may be difficult, but they are possible under the motivation that comes of an understanding of truth." (*Be Thou an Example* [Salt Lake City: Deseret Book Company, 1981], p. 137.)

The scriptures assure us that our labor is not in vain when

125

we serve the Lord. (Malachi 3:14-18.) But I'm told that Charles Manson claimed to labor for the Lord. It is said that Hitler claimed he labored for the Lord. Many who tormented Joseph Smith and the early Saints claimed they labored for the Lord. In fact, many who fight against the Church today claim the same thing. All these labors have proven to be not only vain but wasted and evil as well. I am sure this is why the scriptures say that life eternal is to *know* the only *true* God and Jesus Christ, whom he has sent. (See John 17:3; italics added.) Our labor will not be in vain in the *true* Lord and his *true* church.

"Well . . . " Tiffany was repeating her question. "How can I know what's true?"

For a moment I recalled the year before my mission when I served on the National Executive Board of the Boy Scouts of America. After attending several meetings in New York City, I stood in the airport awaiting my flight home.

"We need your donation," a young man said as he approached me. He was tall, about my build, and was busily pinning a small flower to my lapel.

"I represent the ————," he said, right beneath the sign that read, "We apologize for any inconvenience caused by unauthorized solicitations in this airport." He continued, "We're trying to help young people find purpose in their lives. We need your donation."

I had been approached like this before, just as everyone else has. I felt awkward before, just as everyone else has. And I've given up the coins in my pocket before, just as everyone else has. But this time I did something quite unlike what I had always done before. I said, "I represent the Boy Scouts of America, and we're trying to help young people find purpose in their lives. We need *your* donation."

"Ah, c'mon," he laughed, holding out his cupped hand.

"Come on," I said with a smile, following his pattern. He was shocked.

"You've gotta be kidding," he said.

"Only if you are."

There we stood. Each of us in our particular uniforms, dedicated to our separate organizations. There we stood in the middle of the LaGuardia Airport, each with a hand extended, asking for funds for our individual causes.

How could anyone know the difference between us? By our fruits? At that moment they seemed identical—much like missionaries from many different churches, all walking in pairs and knocking on doors. Our dedication was an indicator of value in our causes, but if someone had to judge between us right then, he or she would have had to look past the fruits and examine our trees. Swinging my thoughts back to Tiffany, I said, "Tell me about Joseph Smith."

She started reciting the well-memorized story, "He was about fourteen, I think, and wanted to dedicate himself to the Lord, but all churches said they were true . . . Hey! that's just like now!" Tiffany had made the discovery.

"So how did Joseph find the truth?" I asked. It was a magic moment—a Camelot moment, when for one brief shining second everything went right.

"If any of you lack wisdom, let him ask of God." (James 1:5.) This is an invitation to Joseph, to Tiffany, to me, to everyone. "And it shall be given" is our promise from heaven.

President Joseph Fielding Smith said, "When a man has the manifestation from the Holy Ghost, it leaves an indelible impression on his soul, one that is not easily erased. It is Spirit speaking to spirit, and it comes with convincing force. A manifestation of an angel, or even the Son of God himself, would impress the eye and mind, and eventually become dimmed, but the impressions of the Holy Ghost sink deeper into the soul and are more difficult to erase." (*Answers to Gospel Questions* [Salt Lake City: Deseret Book Company, 1979], 2:151.)

Though the Spirit will testify of truth wherever and to whatever degree it may be found (see John 14:17, 26) and though Satan tries to imitate the Holy Ghost's witness (see 2 Corinthians 11:14) or make us content with the small influence of the Spirit we might already have, the recognizably different and complete security of the Spirit (the manifestation Joseph Fielding Smith describes) only accompanies recognizable and complete truth.

Wait—I know Mormons who say one thing and do another. I know Mormons who don't go to church on Sunday, and I know Mormons who are dishonest, hypocritical, inactive . . . the list seems endless. Sadly, there are those to whom it applies, but when good fruit has been bird-pecked, damaged by the rain, or even frozen in unseasonable storms, is it the fault of the tree? (See Alma 32:39.) A good cause will stand with or without followers, much like God and quite unlike Satan.

Jesus told the Jews, "If any man will do [God's] will, he shall know of the doctrine, whether it be of God or whether I speak of myself." (John 8:32.) "The Lord told Nephi, "If ye will not harden your hearts, and ask me in faith, believing that ye shall receive, with diligence in keeping my commandments, surely these things shall be made known to you." (1 Nephi 15:11.) Is the cause of Christ worth our consecration? Every person can know! We can be motivated, not by fears or rewards or the obligations and demands placed on us by others, but by the knowledge that God lives and the love that accompanies that knowledge.

One winter morning I woke up early to my alarm that rang at 4:30 A.M. "Why did that thing dare to ring?" I grumbled, until I remembered that I was going to meet a good friend, Steve Bullock, at the temple. We wanted to get through the first session of the day before our classes started.

I dressed, grabbed my books and car keys, and stepped outside into the dark winter morning. I blinked. I couldn't believe what I saw or didn't see—my car was gone! But then, so was the yard, the house, and the neighbor's house. An oatmeal-thick fog combined with the darkness until it seemed as if the whole world had been stolen overnight. Like a blind man, I groped to recover my car in the driveway. I crept across the city like a kid playing hide and seek. The streets to the temple were hiding, and I was seeking them. I honestly could not even see the stoplights change color. Like a first-time Braille reader, I felt my way along. I could only guess at the distances and corners that I thought were right. Nothing was certain. Then suddenly before me, I saw the lights atop the temple. Despite the fog, they were still beaming steadily, illuminating the single, heaven-pointing spire. As though confined by the weather, all the light that usually fills an entire valley seemed to cling around that tower, creating one solid shaft of golden light. The pillar stretched from the temple upward to farther than I could see. This new "light house" enabled me to reach the Lord's house of light without fear, uncertainty, hesitation, or pause.

Is this the same direction and security the Prophet Joseph Smith knew when into his darkness and confusing fog came a pillar of light?

From the spring of 1820 on, the young prophet selflessly dedicated his time, ability, family, and money to the Lord's work. This man gave his life, not only by dying but also by living. He dedicated every hour, day, month, and year to God for his purposes. Was this because he was forced? Because he was indoctrinated and brainwashed? A fanatic in search of attention? A glory-starved shepherd in search of a flock to manipulate? A zealot? A con man? No! Joseph dedicated himself just as I drove—without fear, uncertainty, hesitation, or pause, for in his life, as in my morning, there was a pillar of light. Joseph's fruit is good because his tree is good. His tree is good because it is rooted in complete, eternal, unchanging truth. As the Lord said, "Ye shall know the truth, and the truth shall make you free." (John 8:32.) Joseph knew, and he was free indeed—free from the emptiness of a purposeless life. Free to offer and dedicate himself without the fear of being wrong. Free to work with the security that neither his life nor death would be in vain. Free to know that his sacrifice counted for something. It was not made to an idolatrous stone

129

or man-created defense mechanism, but to a living and loving God.

At Jesus' death, his apostles were lost. One by one, all became disoriented in the fog, for after two and a half years of being sustained and uplifted by Christ's presence, they were now alone, confused, and discouraged.

What changed the doubting, despairing apostles at the crucifixion into the confident, heroic leaders who changed the world? There is but one answer — a pillar of light; the revelation that Christ had risen from the grave. Their faith was not based on a dead Savior but on a living one.

History assures us that those early apostles and Saints had heavy crosses to bear. I'm sure they felt weighted down, imposed upon, and bored with some routine duties. But they took the dead out of their dedication by gaining sure testimonies of truth. Their God was no longer on his own cross but was helping them carry theirs. Suddenly, service projects weren't a chore. Filling a mission became the least they could do. Staying morally clean was not something they *had* to do or *should* do. Now, it was something they *wanted* to do. Yes, suddenly yokes were easy and burdens were light indeed. (See Matthew 11:30.) Did they utter a swear word? No way. Did they look at pornography? Dream on. I can just imagine that they loved waking up for seminary, came to family home evening the minute they were called, and didn't even say "Wait till the commercial!"

It was quite a lesson I learned in that Chilean graveyard a few years back: dedication is a tool — an effective tool, but still just a tool. It is I who must determine to use the tool positively. Through the Spirit, I can know what is true, and as I come to know the Church is indeed true, I can be sure that I'm not wasting my time, money, and efforts.

Elder Maxwell states, "This is a dying world. A living discipleship is attainable, but only if we remember that livingness begets livingness and, therefore, we stay close to the truly living things: the living God, the living Church, the living prophets, and the living scriptures." (*Things as They Really Are*, p. 18.)

President Benson declares, "When you choose to follow Christ, you choose the way, the truth, the life—the right way, the saving truth, the abundant life." (*Ensign*, July 1989, p. 2; see John 14:6.) I too testify that as we dedicate ourselves to Christ, to the ends he approves and authorizes, then our dedication will not be dead but will rise and shine as the Lord has done and still does today.

Brad Wilcox is an instructor in the Elementary Education Department at Brigham Young University. He is the author of four books and has been published in several magazines. He likes peanut M&M's, pepperoni pizza, driving with his car radio turned way up, and his one-time appearance on TV ("Family Feud"). He and his wife, Debi, have two children.

Chapter 13

Learning for Myself

Randal A. Wright

Several years ago, our eight-year-old son came in from playing outside with a huge potted plant. He seemed very excited and told his mother that he was giving it to her as a present. Of course, the first thing we asked him was where he had gotten this special gift. He told us he had found it in a clearing in the woods behind our house. The plant was about five feet tall and very green and healthy. This just didn't make sense to me. It was obvious that someone had taken good care of the plant, and it was in a nice container. After further questioning, we had him show us exactly where he had found the plant. He quickly took us to the spot. We couldn't imagine how the plant had gotten there or who could have taken such good care of it, but we were convinced that our son really had found it behind *our* house.

We decided to put the present in our living room, next to our couch. I must admit that it looked nice sitting there. We have frequent visitors to our home, and several people, including our home teachers and several ward and stake leaders, commented on how nice the plant looked in our living room. But there was something about the plant that never seemed right. Maybe it was the strange smell that was always apparent when you sat near it, or the strange feeling we got as we looked closely at it. It looked more like a healthy weed than anything else. Finally, after about a month, I pulled down a plant book to see if I could identify what kind of plant we had been tending. I flipped through the pages until I finally spotted a plant that looked exactly like ours. I checked very closely to be sure. I even pulled off one of the leaves and put it on the kitchen stove burner to be sure. There was no question about it. We had in our living room a healthy, five-foot-tall marijuana plant. I thought of how good it had looked in the room, and of how many friends and relatives had commented on its beauty. But the fact remained that we not only had an illegal plant in our home, we had actually cared for it. We had the plant destroyed, but I learned for myself from this experience that it is possible to have things in our lives that are not right and yet not even notice them. If we are to make it through life safely, we are going to have to look closely at our actions and our environment to make sure there is nothing inappropriate in them.

As we go through life, we will all make mistakes. But if we learn from our own experience and the experiences of others, we can live happy, useful lives.

Jesus said, "Judge not, that ye be not judged." (Matthew 7:1.) One day after work, I stopped at a self-service gas station. As I was pumping gas into my car, a young man pulled up on the opposite side of the pumps and began to fill his car. I thought as I looked at him, "Poor guy, he doesn't have a chance in life." He had long hair and out-of-style clothing, and he wasn't very comely in his appearance. I found myself looking down on him and actually thinking I was probably better than he was.

After I finished putting the gas in my car, I went to pay the attendant. To my embarrassment, I didn't have enough money to pay the bill. I went back to the car to find some more money. I looked in the glove compartment, under the seat, even under the floor mats — nothing, not one cent! I knew I would have to ask the attendant if I could go home to get more money. Reluctantly, I walked back toward the cashier. About halfway there, I passed the young man I had judged earlier. He smiled and said, "Don't worry about it, man." I thought, "Same to you, smart aleck!" But I had no idea what he was talking about.

Back with the attendant, I explained that I had no money with me. Since I lived only about a mile and a half away, I suggested that I would go home, get some money, and come back to pay her—all within a few minutes. She seemed very calm as she rang up the bills of the other customers, not paying much attention to my dismay. Finally, she said that the young man behind me in line had seen my predicament and paid my gas bill, asking her to tell me not to worry about it.

I hurried outside, ran to his car, and said, "Look, I live just down the road. Please wait here, and I'll bring you the money right back." His only words were, "Don't worry about it, man," and he drove off.

I had never seen this young man before, nor have I seen him since, but he taught me that we should be very careful about judging others. There are many good people in the world who do not necessarily look or act the way we think they should. If we are not careful, we can be lifted up in pride and judge them only by the way they look, or even by the brand of clothing they wear. Let us judge not that *we* be not judged.

Jesus said, "Let your light shine before men, that they may see your good works, and glorify your Father which is in heaven." (Matthew 5:16.) Several years ago when I was serving as a stake missionary, I was privileged to meet a full-time missionary from Utah named Maurice Begay. Elder Begay was a full-blooded Indian and a perfect example of one who had "blossomed as a rose." He showed me, during a "missionary split" one night, why we sometimes need to let our lights shine, even when it's hard. That night as we were out tracting, we drove into a poor area of town. Elder Begay asked me to pull up to a particular mobile home so we could tract it out. I tried to tell him that I was sure the people who lived there would not be interested in the Church, but he would not listen and began to walk up the driveway. I followed him past a couple of junked cars and scattered trash up to the trailer door. I was more than a little nervous as Elder Begay knocked loudly on the door. My confidence sank even more when the man of the house opened the door. He had a cigarette in his mouth, no shirt, tattoos all over his arms, and a scowl on his face. "What do you want?" he asked. I thought, "I want to go home. What do you think I want?" But I said nothing. Elder Begay told him who we were and asked if we could come in and share a message about Christ's visit to the Americas with his family. After a long pause, he invited us in. In his small living room sat his wife and four children. All needed a comb, a bath, a handkerchief, and some better clothing. There was tension in the air as we sat down, and it became obvious that no one was going to speak to us because of their involvement in a TV movie. After a short time, Elder Begay told the family we had a message to share with them. No one responded to his comment. I became more nervous and had a strong desire to get up and leave. The elder tried two more times to talk with the family about the Church, but still they would not reply. After we had sat there for about fifteen minutes, Elder Begay did something that took as much courage as anything I have ever seen. With no warning this young missionary picked up his chair and set it right in front of the TV set, then sat down so the family could not see the movie. Then he reached around and turned off the set. "You don't mind if I turn this off do you?" he asked. There was an eery silence in the room as the family stared at him in disbelief. I have never wanted to run so bad in all my life. After what seemed like an eternity, the man replied, "I guess not; I've already seen that movie anyway." Hearing that brought me more relief than I can describe. That night a young Lamanite missionary taught that family about Joseph Smith and the Restoration. The family was not interested in the Church, just as I had first suspected, but I had witnessed one of the most inspirational events of my life.

That event was more than ten years ago, but I still recall

135

it often, especially when things get hard. I learned for myself that the example we set can affect people for years. When I saw this young elder's light shine before me, it made me want to glorify my Father in heaven through my own actions.

The Lord promised, "If you will ask of me you shall receive; if you will knock it shall be opened unto you." (D&C 11:5.) My wife is a convert to the Church and the only member in her immediate family. She has two younger brothers who have been active members of another faith. Trying to be good missionaries, we prayed for ways to introduce her family to the Church. We invited them to socials and other activities but didn't have much luck.

Finally, we felt the answer to our prayers had come. Her brother Richard agreed to go to a stake dance with us. He was seventeen. We were so excited! We took special pains getting ready so that we felt totally prepared, and we left early to be there on time. We forgot though, that Mormon standard time was in effect. Very few people were there. We introduced Richard to those who were there, but they just said hello and went on their way.

Then the thought hit us: "After praying him here, now what do we do with him?" I have never felt more uncomfortable in my life. Isn't that about the way it is? We pray for something for years, only to find that we don't know what to do with the answer.

As other young people arrived at the dance, we would introduce Richard to them. Again, after a brief "It's good to meet you," they would walk away and dance with the people they already knew, leaving Richard on the sidelines with us. He was close friends with Linda, one of our LDS girls, so we nervously waited for her arrival. As the evening grew into night, a new prayer formed in our hearts, one asking for help to know what to do to help Richard feel welcome and accepted.

Finally Linda came in, walked right up to Richard, and began taking him around introducing him to her friends. What a relief! We began to relax, thinking that all was well—our prayers had again been answered! Our relief was short-lived however, because about fifteen minutes after Linda arrived, Alden walked in. He was the tall, muscular, football-player type, who happened to be Linda's boyfriend. She went straight to him, leaving Richard by himself again. He was soon back at our side looking uncomfortable. The pressure was unreal. We had prayed so diligently for him to come to the activity, never dreaming that he might have a terrible time once he got there.

I looked out on the dance floor and saw Linda and Alden. She was our only hope. I was about to give up and suggest we leave when again our prayers were answered. As this young couple was dancing to a fast song, Alden suddenly made a quick move, and we heard a loud rip from the side-lines. He had ripped the seat of his pants from top to bottom.

Alden lived in another town several miles away. He had no choice but to go home for the night. As soon as he walked out with his hands over his back side, Linda came right over to Richard and never left him for the duration of the dance.

Now, you may think that Alden's ripping his pants was a coincidence, but how many times have you seen something like that happen at a dance? I learned for myself that if we ask, we will receive. The Lord does answer prayers, and sometimes he answers them in unusual ways.

The Lord taught Joseph Smith, "Whether by mine own voice or by the voice of my servants, it is the same." (D&C 1:38.) One of the nicest and most attractive young women I've known is named Monica. She plays the piano, was a straight-A student in high school, and never missed a day in seminary for four years, even though it began at 5:55 A.M. She is a true hundred-percenter in everything she does.

You would think that while she was in high school she would have had all kinds of boys asking her out. She did at first, until they found out her standards. But she took a stand that seriously hurt her social life. She decided to follow what the prophets have counseled regarding dating. First, she refused to date until she was sixteen. Even though many young men wanted to take Monica out before her sixteenth birthday, she followed the Church's counsel. The biggest event in the eighth grade is the end-of-the-year banquet, a formal dinner-dance. Monica was one of only a few girls who attended this special event without a date. Second, she refused to date nonmembers or unworthy members. Living in the mission field and attending a large, predominately nonmember high school, Monica found herself being asked out for dates by nice, popular nonmember boys. That's a tough decision, but she had taken a stand and was determined to stick with it. Monica kept her vow and never went out with a nonmember.

As you can imagine, she ended up having very few dates in high school. She used the time to work on goals, such as sewing, cooking, making good grades, reading the scriptures, obtaining her Young Womanhood Recognition Award, and so on. She was also one of the high school beauties and an officer on the drill team.

Monica did well enough in high school to receive a scholarship to Brigham Young University. After a year she met a young, good-looking returned missionary. They courted and then began a new life together after their marriage in the Washington, D.C., Temple.

Shortly after their wedding, Monica and Benson spoke at our stake's Standard's Night. She wore her white wedding dress and looked beautiful. She told the youth that one of the hardest things she'd ever had to do was go to the eighth-grade banquet alone. It was difficult to turn down dates with nonmembers and sit at home weekend after weekend. But then came her point: "I want to tell all of you here that when I knelt across the altar at the Washington, D.C., Temple and looked into the eyes of a worthy priesthood holder and heard 'married for time and eternity,' I knew it was all worth it!"

Following the Prophet at times seems hard, but if we will do it, there are always bigger and better rewards in the future.

Going against the Prophet may bring temporary pleasure, but it always brings long-term consequences.

As I looked at Monica and Benson that night, I learned for myself that whether words of counsel are from the Lord or his prophet, it is the same. When we follow this counsel, great rewards will come.

You may like cats, and I think that's great. I don't mind cats—as long as they belong to someone else. Once when our sons were small, a good friend had a huge litter of kittens and was not having too much luck giving them away. Knowing of my "unfondness" for the feline species, she knew better than to offer a kitten to me, so she extended the invitation to our four-year-old son Nathan. We politely said, "Thank you," and went on our way. What else could I say, since the kitten had been a gift?

Nathan loved that cat so much that he dubbed her "Miss Mormon." How can you turn your kid down when he gives an animal a name like that? I still didn't like the cat rubbing against my leg—I didn't even want her in the house! In time, things changed somewhat. As the kitten grew, I saw how much fun the boys had with her, and I began to enjoy her a little myself. I kind of liked having her around.

Then one day Nathan couldn't find Miss Mormon anywhere. We looked all over the neighborhood. After several days, my wife was coming home from a meeting and saw our cat on the side of the road, dead. She had apparently been hit by a car.

I told Nathan what had happened and that we would need to go pick her up so we could bury her. He went in and got a small plastic garbage sack and bravely took my hand as we walked down the road in the direction my wife had pointed out. When we found our cat, she was stiff and bloated. Her tongue was hanging out, and her tail was sticking straight up into the air.

I wanted to teach my son a lesson, so I said, "It's your cat. You put her in the bag." But she was so stiff he couldn't do it. I tried to use my foot to help him out a little, but we didn't have much luck.

Finally I saw it was no use. The cat was too big and stiff to get into the sack, so Nathan just wrapped the bag around the cat and carried it. It was quite a sight. Our small son, eyes red from crying, carrying a huge, stiff cat—its tongue sticking out and tail sticking out from under the bag.

As we made our way down the road toward home, Nathan could barely carry the cat. As we passed by our neighbor's home, Mrs. Cooper waved at us from her yard. She took one look at Nathan's bundle and burst out laughing. I looked down at that big, stiff cat that he loved—it was almost as big as he was right then—and almost laughed myself. But then I saw the big tears rolling down Nathan's cheeks.

We finally arrived home and buried the cat in the backyard. Several months later, the Coopers moved from our neighborhood. Three years went by, and one day Nathan was told that Mrs. Cooper was coming for a visit. He said, "I don't like Mrs. Cooper." "Why not?" I asked. "Because she laughed at me when Miss Mormon got killed." He had remembered that incident vividly for three years.

Empathy and understanding are very important. I learned for myself that people are hurt and may resent us if we are not sensitive to their feelings. We should remember to treat people as we want to be treated ourselves.

Joseph Smith once wrote, "Shall we not go on in so great a cause? Go forward and not backward. Courage, brethren; and on, on to the victory!" (D&C 128:22.) While attending a youth conference in a southern state recently, I listened as several youth bore their testimonies. Michelle, a beautiful black girl, walked up to the podium and began unfolding her life's goal—to be a recording artist—and the events that had recently happened in her pursuit of this goal.

She said that she had worked hard, and finally it appeared as if her dream would come true. Representatives came to her home with a song and offered her the opportunity to make her first record. Michelle felt like jumping up and down she was so excited! But then she began reading the words to the song that had been written especially for her, and a sick feeling came over her. She felt her new-found dream slipping away. The lyrics were not up to Church standards. What would you do? They weren't too bad, but she didn't feel good about performing something that went against her values and beliefs.

There was a silence in the room, and then Michelle looked up at the recording company representative and said, "I can't sing this song. Its words go against what I believe in." The people tried to convince her that one song wouldn't matter. Michelle knew the answer, but it hurt badly. Her parents said, "Michelle, this is the big opportunity that you have been waiting for. Go ahead and sing it. Don't throw away this chance."

But some things in life cannot be bought. Michelle stood up for what she knew was right. The answer was no. She could not and would not sing that song. Sometimes it isn't easy to stand up for what you believe in. The representative left, and Michelle went to her room and cried herself to sleep that night. But she felt good that she had had the courage to stand up for what was right.

Two days later someone knocked at the front door. There stood the same people who had visited her before. They explained that they had changed the lyrics just for Michelle, and that they still wanted her to sing it. This young woman, who stood up for what was right when everything and everybody around her said to compromise her standards, now has her first record out and will probably have many more to come. I was so proud of this young girl. Tears came to my eyes as I heard her story of great courage. That day I learned for myself that when we go forth in a great cause and have courage, the Lord will bless us and the victory will be ours.

The Lord has said, "Behold and lo, mine eyes are upon

you, and the heavens and earth are in mine hands." (D&C 67:2.)

Recently I visited with a seminary teacher in a central state. He shared with me a story of a former seminary student named Mike. One day after class, this big football player came up to his seminary teacher and said, "We're having a keg party Friday night in the canyon. You should come." Then he turned around laughing with his friends and began walking out of the class. Well, what would you have said if you had been the teacher? This teacher said, "You bet, I'll be there! Where are you going to be and what time does it start?" This took Mike by surprise, and he said, "You're not really going to come, are you?" He looked afraid and almost pleading now. No longer was he trying to impress his friends—he was trying to get himself out of a tight situation.

There are lots of Mikes out there, probably some in your school—Mr. tough guy during the week, goes to keg parties on the weekends, then sits in church on Sunday. They seem to want to impress their friends more than they want to keep the commandments.

This loving seminary teacher continued the conversation. He said, "No, Mike, I won't come to your party on Friday. I can tell you really don't want me there, but I'd like you to do me a favor." By now Mike probably would have done anything to get the pressure off. The teacher continued, "I want you to promise me that Friday night as you go to take a drink, you will keep your eyes open." Mike answered, "Well, I guess so. But, why?" "Because when you lean your head back to drink your beer, I want you to look up in the sky so you'll remember something. Will you remember as you look up that our Heavenly Father is watching you? He will be looking down into your eyes. And, do you know what, Mike? I don't think you'll have the nerve to drink that beer, knowing Heavenly Father will be watching you. Will you do that, Mike? Keep your eyes open?" With that, they parted company.

The next Monday, Mike came into seminary and said to

his teacher, "You ruined my whole weekend." "Why, what happened?" his teacher asked. "Well, I went to the party and took a glass of beer from the keg. Just as I got the glass to my lips, I remembered what you had said about keeping my eyes open, and so I did. Then I looked up and imagined Heavenly Father watching me. I've never felt so uncomfortable in all my life. You ruined my whole night," Mike concluded. But he said it with a twinkle in his eye and a tone of thankfulness.

I learned for myself from this experience that it helps to remember that a loving Heavenly Father is watching our actions. This can be a great protection from the temptations we face.

King Benjamin said, "When ye are in the service of your fellow beings ye are only in the service of your God." (Mosiah 2:17.) Brandie was so excited. She had been invited by her best friend to go to Astroworld, a large amusement park in Houston, Texas. This outing would be a kind of going-away party for her friend, whose family would be moving soon. She ran into the house to tell her mom. Everyone was happy for her. Then they looked at the calendar and realized that date was already taken. A youth service project had been planned for that date, and Brandie knew that she would have to choose a church activity over the amusement park. She suddenly wasn't happy at all.

The morning of the service project, Brandie got up begrudgingly, pulled on her work clothes, and headed for the widow's house the group would be painting. I got there about mid-morning to find Brandie on top of the house, hot and sweaty in the August heat. I asked her if she was having fun, just to kid her a little, knowing that she had been upset about not being able to go with her friend. "Yes, I am," came her reply. "I really am. I'm so glad I'm here. We should do this more often." She had paint from head to toe and was dipping her brush into a bucket to finish off the last little bit of the eaves. At first I thought she was being sarcastic, but I soon realized that she was serious. She really was glad to be a part of the service project.

All the youth took great pride in their work. Since that special day, many of the youth have driven past the house several times to see the difference that coat of paint made on the widow's home and to remember the good feelings that came from their act of service.

The youth received the following letter from the widow: "I want to thank all of the young people and their parents for painting my house. I still go outside and walk all the way around just to look at it and be sure it isn't something I'd dreamed about. It's all true, and there are young people in this world who are taught to love and serve elderly people who can't do everything for themselves. I pray the Lord will bless each and every one. I hope they remember, too, that in doing for 'the least of these,' we are serving him."

I learned for myself, just as Brandie had, that when we're in the service of our fellow beings, we are only in the service of our God.

The Lord said, "Fear not to do good, my sons, for whatsoever ye sow, that shall ye also reap; therefore, if ye sow good ye shall also reap good for your reward." (D&C 6:33.) During our son Nathan's freshman year in high school, he was asked to participate with two classmates in a three-part speech. He was excited for this part of his speech class until he found out what their topic would be. The three youth were assigned to present the positive side of a woman's right to an abortion. Nathan came home quite upset. The other two in his team didn't want to talk on that any more than he did. They had asked the teacher for another topic, but her reply was, "You can give this topic or get a zero — take your choice." They asked if they could give their speech on the pro-life side of the issue, but she said no.

After talking among themselves, the two non-members decided they'd just go ahead with the assigned topic, even though they didn't agree with the pro-abortion issue. We had taught Nathan to obey and respect his teachers, so he felt real turmoil in this matter. By the time he came home that afternoon, he needed some parental intervention.

"Do others know you are a Mormon?" we asked. "Sure, everyone in the class! And I'm the only member of the Church in this class," he replied. "What if someone gets an abortion someday because of something I say in my speech about abortion being okay?" These were the ideas going through his mind, but on the other hand, he knew he couldn't afford a zero since this was a major part of his grade.

I brought my files on the abortion issue home. Nathan began thumbing through the papers and came across some vivid colored pictures depicting the horrors of abortion. This had a tremendous impact on him, and helped him come up with his decision. He said, "I'm not giving the speech, whether she gives me a zero or not. I just can't speak favorably about something that goes against everything I believe in."

The next day he went to his speech class and politely explained to his teacher that he would not be giving the speech on the positive aspects of abortion. There was a long silence as he looked down at his teacher sitting at her desk. The silence was broken when he said, "And I don't want a zero either." Then he sat down, leaving her with a decision of her own to make.

We knew Nathan had done the right thing, but we didn't want him to fail this portion of his class either. The next day after school, he came in and said, "Guess what the new topic is for my speech: Why abortion should be illegal." He was so excited—and relieved!

The next week, Nathan gave a powerful pro-life speech after his two teammates had presented the pro-abortion side of the issue. He noticed several tears in his classmates' eyes when he was presenting his speech, and various students talked to him afterward about his statements. The teacher was visibly irritated with his remarks. She was critical of his presentation, especially mentioning that he got the class too emotionally involved.

A short time later, we received an invitation to attend a year-end academic awards presentation at the high school. Nathan makes good grades, so we figured he'd be receiving an honor in biology or algebra. The names were read off for both of those subjects with no mention of our son's name. Toward the end of the event, we heard Nathan's name called out. We weren't really paying much attention to this category—theater arts, debate, speech—because we knew he didn't have a chance in this area. But, Nathan was going to pick up his award—the honor award for ninth-grade speech class. We were totally surprised! Apparently the teacher had reconsidered her opinion and ended up admiring him for his stand. Nathan learned for himself that he need not fear doing good and that if he sows good, he will reap good for his reward.

The Lord said, "If it so be that you should labor all your days in crying repentance unto this people, and bring, save it be one soul unto me, how great shall be your joy." (D&C 18:15.) A few months ago our family received a letter from Japan. Since we didn't know anyone who lived there, we were all curious about the contents of the letter. I opened it and found a letter and a picture from a beautiful Japanese girl. We couldn't imagine who she was and how she had gotten our address or why she would be writing to our family. The letter read: "Dear Wright Family:

"How do you do? My name is Chikako Iba. I am Japanese. I met the sister missionaries on the street and the next day I went to church. This was three weeks ago. The sisters taught me about the plan of salvation and the church. I learned a lot of new things.

"I would like to introduce myself. There are six people in my family (father, mother, little brother, grandfather and grandmother). I am 20 years old, and am a student at the

Yamagata Women's Community College. I study Japanese Literature.

"I will graduate soon, so school tests are soon. I am studying very much. Japan is very cold. Is Vidor, Texas, cold? Please take care of yourself.

"I live in Iwate-Ken. Iwate-Ken is very nice. Please come and see me. I was given a Book of Mormon from your family. Thank you very much. It is a real treat to me. The Book of Mormon is a help to know the truth. [Then it hit me. About a year earlier our family had written our testimonies and placed them in copies of the Book of Mormon with a family picture and sent them to a Japanese Mission.]

"Once again, thank you for the Book of Mormon and helping me to know the truth. I was baptized on January 22, 1989, at the Yamagata Ward. I am very happy."

I can't tell you the joy our family received from that letter. To think that with such little effort on our part, a young girl thousands of miles away had joined the Church. We learned for ourselves the great joy that comes from sharing the gospel with others.

The Lord told Martin Harris, "Learn of me, and listen to my words; walk in the meekness of my Spirit, and you shall have peace in me." (D&C 19:23.) In our world there is much trouble and sorrow. The teenage years can be especially trying for many. But there are many helps available if we will take advantage of them. We have the scriptures, prayers, our families, friends, church leaders, youth programs, seminary, temple trips, youth conferences, and many other things to help us. Many youth fail to catch the vision of how these aids can help. Their scriptures lay unopened, and they do not attend Church meetings and activities as well as they should be. Some fail to attend youth programs and conferences because these cost money, and they are unwilling to work and sacrifice to attend. Some go to these programs only for the fun and fail to catch the vision of what they can learn. Fortunately, there are others who make any sacrifice required to

147

learn about the important things in life. I would like to tell you about two of these youth.

When I first met Adam, I misjudged him badly. I thought because of his stylish clothes and hair that he was at the youth conference for all the wrong reasons. But I was wrong. Although he had come to the conference to have fun and meet new people, he had also come seeking a testimony. He sincerely wanted to learn. Because he was where he was supposed to be for the right reasons, he got the peace he sought. After one of the youth conference speakers had spoken on the life of Christ, this young man decided he must do as Joseph Smith had done. When he returned home from the conference, he prayed for divine guidance. He wrote a poem that described his experience and shared it with me.

> Tonight I felt something I've never felt
> While at bedside on my knees I knelt
> To the Father, a silent prayer I dealt.
> My knees hit the floor, and the bed gave a squeak.
> The flesh was willing but the spirit was weak.
> In the silent night, I heard my mind speak:
> Our Father in heaven—Canst thou hear my prayer?
> Does my muffled cry pierce thy heavenly air?
> Canst thou lift me from my earthly care?
>
> Did thy son to the world of old descend?
> Has thy church been restored to the earth again?
> Is it true what they say? That's all—amen.
> Does God really exist? Would an answer come?
> Could my feeble prayer reach his mighty kingdom?
> Could an infidel receive revelation?
> In the silent night—I yawned and sighed,
> Then an answer came as a peaceful tide.
> My heart did swell and hours I cried.
> The confusion fled, and all my doubts died.
> I had prayed with faith as the scriptures had said.
> Oh, that feeling forever—that prayer in my head

Our Father in heaven—tonight by my bed.

Because Adam, as a teenager, went to that conference to learn about the Savior and the important things in life, he learned for himself, just as the scriptures have promised.

One of the most beautiful teenage girls I know is named Chelsey. Not only is she beautiful on the outside but on the inside as well. I have never met a girl her age who tried harder to learn about the Savior and to be like him.

When Chelsey had a chance to attend a youth conference in her area in Texas, she began planning to attend. Although she comes from a large family and money is tight, she worked hard to earn the money to go. Like others, she went to meet new friends and to have fun. But that wasn't her main reason for attending—she want to learn more about the Savior. Because she went with that intent, she got her desire. She wrote the following letter after the event.

"The conference was the best spiritual experience I've had in my whole life, other than the temple trips I've made. The classes were extremely inspirational. Each class seemed to help me with different problems I was having. I know what they mean about being at the right place at the right time. Things that I've been hearing all my life just seemed to make more sense when I heard them at the conference. For example, I heard, "When ye have done it unto the least of these my brethren, ye have done it unto me" in one of the talks. For some reason it seemed to take on a different meaning. I've always thought it applied to service, but I realized that when we are mean to a person, it's like we're being mean to Christ. After I thought about it, it really made me want to be nicer, sweeter, and more compassionate toward people. While I was there, we got to watch two slide shows about Christ, and it had beautiful music playing with it. I don't guess I've ever realized how much Jesus really loves me as an individual until I saw these slide shows. It made me want to try harder to get back to him. It just gives me chills to think about him embracing me and saying, "Well done, thou good and faithful servant." I think the conference helped me realize how much harder I need to work to be able to live with him again. I love my Savior with all my heart, and there's nothing I'd rather do than spend eternity with my family and with God in the celestial kingdom. The testimony meeting was really spiritual. It just seemed to pull us all closer together. This conference was one of the best experiences I've had in my whole life."

Adam and Chelsey learned for themselves the great joy and peace that come from learning more about the Savior. As you go through life, I hope you will learn for yourself what is really important. And if you learn nothing else, I hope you will learn that Joseph Smith was a prophet, that the Church is true, that we have a living prophet today, that Jesus Christ is our Savior, and that we have a loving Heavenly Father. If we learn these things for ourselves, then we will find real joy and purpose in life.

Randal A. Wright is an institute director and regional coordinator for the Church Educational System. He was the founder and editor of Mormon Sport Magazine *and has published a book,* Families in Danger. *He and his wife, Wendy, have five children, and they live in Vidor, Texas.*